My
FATHER'S
PRAYERS

A Refugee's Continuing Search for Freedom

PETER LUMAJ, ESQ.

PAGE PUBLISHING, INC.
New York, NY

First originally published by Page Publishing, Inc. 2019

ISBN 978-1-64544-502-9 (Paperback)
ISBN 978-1-64544-504-3 (Digital)

Printed in the United States of America

PART I
PETER'S STORY

Peter Lumaj was born and raised in communist Albania. Lack of freedom and opportunity in his homeland encouraged Peter and his three brothers to escape oppression and settle in the United States. They left behind their parents and their seven other siblings, who suffered severe persecution at the hands of the communist government.

Once in the United States, Peter learned English and enrolled in the City University of New York. While attending college, Peter worked as a porter and a doorman to support his family and to pay for his education. Peter went on to graduate cum laude with a BA in political science. Later, Peter enrolled in the Benjamin N. Cardozo School of Law. While attending law school, he worked as a fraud investigator in the Giuliani administration.

In 2014, Peter was selected as the Republican nominee for Connecticut secretary of state. In the 2014 general election, he is credited with running one of the closest races for statewide office in recent history in Connecticut.

In 2018, he sought the Republican nomination governor in the state of Connecticut, he fell short three delegates at the Republican Convention, narrowly missing the threshold to automatically qualify for a spot on the primary ballot. Rather than pursue a petition process for ballot access, Lumaj withdrew from the race and returned to the private sector.

Currently, Peter is a small businessman, a practicing attorney, and the owner of the Law Offices of Lumaj. In addition, Lumaj makes major media appearances as a Republican political strategist, including Fox News, Sky News, FOX 61, i24NEWS, etc. He remains involved in national, state, and local politics and is widely recognizable as a major force within the conservative movement within the Connecticut Republican Party.

Peter Lumaj resides in Fairfield, Connecticut. He is married to his wife, Mary, and they have three children: Frank, Amy, and Larisa.

www.peterlumaj.com

Part 1

GROWING UP IN TYRANNY

Communism is cruel; it kills, it depresses a society, it impoverishes the people, and it makes all aspects of life rigid, but it unleashes the human spirit like no other force on earth. The time I spent in Albania was full of misfortune and misery, but without its enduring desolation, I might not have ever had the courage to make the most important journey of my life, a journey that led me to the United States. This is my story.

I grew up in Dedaj, a small Catholic village in Northern Albania. The area was isolated, the life was tribal, and the people were hard and worn; in fact, it could easily be said that the current state of Dedaj is not too different from the Dedaj that I left in 1989. Dedaj is part of a region known as Shkrel, which, in conjunction with four other neighboring regions, Hot, Kelemend, Kastrat, and Grunde, constitute a political district known as Malesi e Madhe or the highlands. My family, the Lumaj clan, was considered to be one of the largest and most powerful families in the region.

During the 1940s, when the Albanian communists began their military campaign of control and conquer, my family stood in their way and fought them until the bitter end—an end that would almost lead to the complete extinction of my family. After the communist regime came to power, my family's land, properties, and livestock were confiscated for opposing the regime. Further, all homes were burned to the ground, and the majority of the male members of my family were publicly executed as a political message to all persons opposing the communist government.

As the communist regime's powers became stronger, the people of Albania became destitute. Families were forced to stand in line for daily rations. We stood in line each and every day for miniscule rations of bread, milk, sugar, marmalade, and cheese. Meats, fruits, and vegetables were not available to the general public, but they were available to the local communist officials.

My father was a quiet man, a devout Christian, and a steadfast anti-communist. He worked hard, seven days a week without complaint, and was completely and totally devoted to his large family (eleven children—six boys and five girls) and to his faith. He was, by far, the most influential figure in my life.

Life in Albania was simple enough for a young boy, but there were many things I could not comprehend until I was older. Growing up I never understood why we had to live many aspects of our lives in secret. We were instructed by my father to never disclose that we said prayers at home and on no occasion discuss the content of the radio and the discussions taking place inside of our house. I don't think at that time any of us ever questioned why. We just knew not to disobey our father.

Each and every night, my father would be accompanied home by my uncle Gjek (Jack), who joined him for Albanian whisky (raki) and discussion. As both men would enter our home, they began their routine; all doors leading outside of the house were locked, all windows would be closed, all the household curtains would be pulled down, and the children would be dismissed to the bedroom. When all was safe, the radio was turned on. The Voice of America was my father's preferred station, and I can still hear the distinctive introductory voice of Elez Byberaj in my head. "You are listening to Voice of America from the Washington of the United States," the radio would whisper.

I must have been roughly thirteen years old when my father first invited me to join him and my uncle to listen to the radio with them. I didn't know it then, but this event would greatly impact the remainder of my life and forge the person who I am today; but at that time, I was just excited to spend time with my father and be treated like a man—a big achievement for a boy my age. I was hooked, and before long, I joined in on my father and uncle's routine almost every night, even though I had little understanding of what was being listened to and discussed.

One night, as we had finished listening to a program on Radio Vatican, spoken in the Albanian language, my father began to educate me on the speaker of the program. He informed me that the speaker was Father Daniel Gjecaj, an Albanian priest who resided in Italy, who was best known for his harsh words against the Albanian communist regime. This conversation was my introductory lesson into truly understanding communism.

"Daniel Gjecaj is an anti-communist," he said, and I was stunned. Being only thirteen, I did not know how to comprehend this news; I could not fathom that anybody could be anti-communist. We had spent our entire youths learning about the success of communism in school and the failures of capitalism abroad. We were subjected to political indoctrination at an early age, and it was implemented in all parts of our lives outside the household. My father recognizing the look of dire confusion on my face, and he explained further.

"You see. So Albania has a political regime called communism, which means control, control of the individual. When God created men, he wanted them to be free. He gave them certain rights such as life and liberty. He, God, in the men's spirit, created a yearning for freedom, and no other men should take that away from us. When a man, who claims to be our leader, tell us that our rights come from the government, he is trying to play god. God gives us these rights. Our rights do not come from the government but from God. In the Western world, people wrote constitutions to make sure that their governments do not get too strong."

Still stunned from his explanation, I began to realize that my father was an anti-communist too. I inquired further, "What is a constitution?" I asked.

He looked back at me with loving eyes and the big smile a parent often gives to their ignorant child and said, "A constitution is a document, something that is written in most places, where the wise men of those countries enumerated the powers of their governments, telling the government what it could and could not do." He spoke of examples and told me about a faraway place called the United States of America.

It was a name I had heard before. A name I learned and taught to me as an enemy to our people, by my teachers in school. My history teacher, Ms. Muhamet, had taught the pupils of my class that this place, the United States of America, was an intolerable place, a place where government forsakes its own people. She told us that it was a bad place riddled with unemployment, poverty, no health insurance, and the country had imperialistic tendencies. She further explained that people in the United States did not possess our freedoms and that their leaders were corrupt and unconscionable.

My father continued, "America is the place where people from all over the world go in search of their dreams. These people who go there are usually persecuted by their own governments and leave for America, searching for freedom and realizing dreams. This is a place where you can be all you can as long as you work hard and play by the rules. The government does not penalize you for what your parents or grandparents did."

"One can even be a lawyer?" I asked my father.

"Yes, son, yes," he responded.

I had always wanted to be a lawyer.

That same evening, after falling asleep, I had a dream about one day living in this faraway place. I dreamed that I was flown to America on the back of a large bird, leaving the world I knew behind. In my dream, I learned how to speak their language, sing their songs, play their games, frequent their nightlife, and date their girls. I dreamed of attending university, learning their laws, and practicing law in a large city. It was a dream I will never forget but also a dream I could not share with anyone because it could and would cause me and my family trouble.

The next day, while attending school, I barely associated with the other children and participated in class. I was exuberant with the dream and the conversation I had the night before, but I was scared that the joy I was feeling could land me in trouble. My joy had to remain with me and me alone.

Later that same day, almost as if it was planned, my teacher, Ms. Muhamet, spoke of the evils of the United States again. I listened and said nothing, fantasizing still of my dream the night before. Ms. Muhamet, realizing my lack of attention, called upon me to embarrass me in front of the other students. She asked me to tell the class who the enemies of Albania were. This was an exercise often used to implement the propaganda of the regime. I recited back to her, as I was taught in school: Yugoslavia, China, Russia, Greece, Italy, France, England. But for some reason or another, I forgot the United States. Maybe my mistake was a subconscious thought after the conversation and dream the night before. I did not want to believe that the United States was our enemy.

"What about the United States of America?" she said. "Is it not our biggest enemy? I explained this to you before. How come you don't remember it?"

"Oh, yes," I said. "You are right. The United States of America is our biggest enemy. They are imperialistic, and the government does not help its people. They have no jobs, no food, etc."

"Very good," she said and asked me to pay attention to her lecture.

I skipped work that day, eager to return home and ask my father additional questions. At that time, all children were expected to participate in work cooperatives to help build the socialist experiment; just another form of government indoctrination that advocated the ideals of communism—work to your ability and take to your need. The simple reality was, however, pure political propaganda and free labor for the government. Skipping work had serious consequences, but at that time, I didn't care. I craved conversation with my father, and I was too excited to wait. As my father came home and walked inside, I could barely contain my excitement. I waited anxiously as he poured a drink, caught up on the day's events with my mother, and tuned his radio. As the familiar voice whispered across the room, I picked a seat directly next to him on our family's couch and lay down, concentrating intently on the content of the radio program. I hated our couch, essentially a poorly crafted wooden bench without any real cushion, but tonight I didn't care. I felt like a man and was ready to listen and learn. When the program concluded, I had even more questions than the night before. In fact, on this particular night, I had so many questions that I fell asleep on that awful couch midconversation and spent the reminder of the night there. This was only the second night of education bestowed upon me by my father, but it became a routine that I actively participated in each and every night form there on out. A routine which I was really enjoying. Father, son, and uncle talking politics, and it made me feel like a grown man.

I learned a great deal from my father and uncle about all aspects of life over the course of these evening chats, but their brash verbal protests against the government remained in my mind most prevalently. My father explained to me that communism punishes achievement and rewards failure and mediocrity, that our government fails the individual because even though it advocates equality, it only protects the elite. He stated that communists speak of the government as the solution to every problem that we face because it serves to consolidate their power, which was, indeed, the real problem that we faced. He educated me that communists were responsible for the attack on our faith and were responsible for creating the atheist state, which is why we had to pray in secret. Communists were threatened by all religion because the commitment to God threatened the power and commitment to our state leaders. All religion was outlawed, but practicing Muslims were seen more favorably than Catholics because the major Catholic families had opposed the initial spread of communism. In fact, communists often publicly described Catholics as enemies of the state and backward thinkers.

He lamented that communism stood in direct contradiction to our family values, our Albanian traditions, and even the purpose of man. He viewed all aspects of the government as overreaching and even thought that all people working within it were sadistic people and control freaks. He frequently told me that any government that exercises control over the means of production, distribution, and exchange would eventually turn their own populations into slaves, which is what all Albanians now were. He believed that people might even have to stand up and fight even when there was no chance of victory because it was better to perish than to live as slaves.

My uncle Jack often talked about a British leader, who had opposed communism and socialism by telling his people that "Socialist policy is abhorrent to British ideas on freedom. There is to be one state to which all are to be obedient in every act of their lives. This state, once in power, will prescribe for everyone: where they are to work, what they are to work at, where they may go, and what they may say, what views they are to hold, where their wives are to queue up for the state ration, and what education their children are to receive. A socialist state could not afford to suffer opposition. No socialist system can be established without political police. They would have to fall back on some form of gestapo."

Part 2

HIGH SCHOOL YEARS

A fter eighth grade, I was the first one in my family to be allowed by the government to attend a regular boarding high school in the city of Koplik. It was a big deal to attend one of these institutions because for years, my family had been barred from similar places of higher education because of our family's strong opposition to communism in the 1940s. All the slots to attend these institutions had been reserved to communist-supporting families. Little did they know that at this point, I was as vigorously anti-communist as my father.

High school in Albania had little to do with education; the only education we ever truly received was instruction in communist indoctrination. Our typical day started by rising at 6:00 a.m. and eating a small breakfast consisting of bread, marmalade, and a cup of tea at 6:45 a.m. After breakfast, all students were forced to attend a "political orientation" class, where usually a middle-aged communist party official would speak to us about the benefits of living under a communist regime and the dangers of capitalist societies. After our daily dose of brainwashing propaganda, we were allowed to attend regular classes, where at least two classes per day were entirely focused on the history of the Communist Party and the political theory behind the rise of Marxism and Leninism.

After classes ended for the day, lunch was served. Lunch usually consisted of dry rice called pilaf or soup and a slice of bread. When we celebrated holidays, usually the birthday of a particular communist leader or the Albanian defeat of Germany and Italy in World War II, we were served macaroni or some type of meat that primarily consisted of bones. After lunch, we partook in personal study time, where, again, we read more about the benefits of communism. Supper was served later in the evening and mirrored morning breakfast—a slice of bread, marmalade, and a cup of tea.

High school was where I learned that I couldn't trust anybody. I and almost everybody I knew from my time there lived in complete and utter fear. It was well-known that some of our peers, other students, who came from communist-trusted families were actively collecting information and documenting conversations of the student body to use against us. This so-called intelligence was presented to and documented by the directors of the school who all were official Communist Party members and who were often nonpracticing Muslims who hated Catholics.

I was called into the directors' office more than once during my time in high school career, and I can remember being very frightened each and every time. As we were called in for our interrogations with the directors, a police officer was always present. We would be asked about our conversations with other students, our political beliefs, and our willingness to cooperate with school officials in rooting out traitors. Failure to comply with their demands and their suspicion of your own personal anti-communist activity would result in brutal physical punishment from the officer in the room. Their lengthy interrogations and brutal use of force to get the information they wanted convinced many throughout the school that the communists even knew our most personal thoughts.

One particular time I visited the directors' office stands out. I was a sophomore in high school when I was called in the office to meet with a director to discuss my family. I entered the room to a short, very fat, bald-headed man; I remember this so distinctly because I thought to myself that he looked very well-fed in a time where almost the entire country was starving. His hefty weight suggested that he must hold a prominent role within the Communist Party. In fact, we often joked in school and called the party officials "little, fat people" because they generally came from Southern Albania, a non-Catholic region of the country were people are genetically shorter and had access to the luxuries of party leadership. The director stared at me intently and asked me to sit down. He informed me that the local police officer wished to meet with me to discuss my relationship with my immediate family and the content of the discussions taking place within my family's house. He wished to know if my father was listening to any enemy radio stations and if he was actively speaking out against the Communist Party and leaders to family members or the public.

Terrified that the government might, in fact, know what was transpiring at my household, I froze for a moment, but then an image of my father came to mind. My father was strong, resolute in his beliefs, and brave; like him, I would not surrender or submit to these people. I collected my thoughts as quickly as I could, found my most sarcastic voice, and informed both the director and the officer that no such activities were transpiring at my household. Furthermore, I insisted that I was thankful to the party for allowing me the opportunity to attend regular high school and that my family was living happily. The director was furious with me; however, much to my surprise, no subsequent beating followed suit. He yelled at me to leave and instructed me to report any suspicious activity seen or heard. He reminded me that it was my duty and obligation to Albania and the party to notify him.

Part 3

LIFE IN TIRANA

After attending high school, the government directed me to the Agriculture Institute (AI) in Tirana, the capitol of Albania, to study agronomy. This was an official directive of the government in which neither I or my family had any decision. The Agriculture Institute was not part of the University of Tirana (UT), which was the only university in Albania at that time. The University of Tirana had roughly ten thousand students that came from trusted communist families, whereas the Agriculture Institute had a little over seven thousand students from rural village areas. My time in Tirana was terrible. I hated the institution, despised my field of study, and loathed the way in which students at Agriculture Institute were treated; we were at best second-class slaves in the eyes to everyone else. In Tirana, I was the lowest of the low in the eyes of the elites. I was a Northern Albanian Catholic, raised in a small rural area, and from a family with a long line and history of anti-communist rabble-rousers.

Life was different yet the same in many respects. I was now considered an adult in the eyes of much of my society; however, the government still treated us all like we were children. There was little excess freedom, and we were still being indoctrinated daily to communist propaganda through additional political orientation classes taught at AI. The whole thing was starting to become a joke, and by this point, many other students were starting to see it too.

Communism was still strong, powerful, and present, but discord among the students was starting to rise, and the lies of communism were starting to be seen. Dissidence was everywhere.

Many of the students were as unsatisfied with the regime as I was and were equally as outspoken; but caution always seemed to prevent any major exploit from taking place. The government was still feared by many, and our convictions, no matter how noble or true, were often squashed by the prospect of death.

The nonconformity of the student body was starting to worry the government, and the necessity to stop the resistance became one of the government's top priorities. My time at AI saw an influx of little, fat people or agents of the feared Sigurimi political police interjecting themselves into all aspects of campus life. Like all government and party appointees in Albania, Sigurimi agents all came from trusted and true communist families. Like us, these agents were trained in their respective field in Tirana, at the Sigurimi School, with a focus on protection and defense of the Communist Party from all enemies, foreign and domestic. The Sigurimi were so effective at penetrating the student body that most students could not recognize their true identity until they would make an arrest or they would testify against another student they suspected of promoting agitation or Western propaganda, or of being anti-communist.

One of the most prominent little, fat people on campus was Sigurimi Agent Vegji Halili, a Muslim communist from Kukes, Albania. When Mr. Halili ran into me "accidentally" one day, I knew the agents had started following my activities and that I was under serious suspicion. I remember our encounter as clear as day. Halili started out our conversation by announcing his disgust with the Kosovars in the student body, a confusing statement from a communist agent because Kosovars were natural communist allies. Then it hit me. He was trying to set me up.

"Never trust a Kosovar," he told me.

I was tempted to inquire further and ask why not, but I knew better. He recognized that I knew he was an agent; who was I to question his knowledge and judgment?

He continued, "Would you like to know why?"

"No," I replied. "Your word suffices because it comes from you," I said in a sarcastic voice.

He pushed me further.

"I don't know much about Kosovars," I told him.

He explained that the "Kosovars had escaped from Kosovo in early and mid-1980s because they were having religious problems with the surrounding Serbs. Kosovars were Muslims mainly left behind by the Ottoman Empire, whereas Serbs were Christians."

So much about his historical knowledge, I said to myself. "Interesting," I replied and informed him that I had to leave. While very little came of this whole encounter, it was my first distinct sign that I was running out of time.

A few weeks later, I saw Halili again, but this time he didn't see me. It was about 10:30 p.m., and I was walking down the hallway of building number 5, returning from an evening with friends. I watched as Halili placed a sign on the bathroom door that said, "Out of order. Must not be used," and walked inside and locked it behind him. I decided to follow him, as best as I could, to see what was going on. I walked down the hallway to the other side of the bathroom, climbed the wall to the vent, and began to listen in. Sure enough, I was able to hear the conversation clearly; two men were talking about a recent issue on campus that I was all too familiar with. To this day, I could not identify who the other voice was, but that gentleman was informing to Halili the identities of two men responsible for the defacement of a portrait of Ramiz Aliza, the prime minister and current leader of the Communist Party. The identities mention were myself and my best friend and roommate, Niko. The informant was right, we were responsible.

After overhearing the conversation, I jumped down from my perch and slowly returned to the room to tell Niko about the encounter. He was calm, cool, and collected; a thinker and a vigilant anti-communist like me. I trusted Niko with my life, and I was confident that if we were caught that he would hold firm and not betray me. I was also confident that he felt the same way about me. After our discussion, I followed Niko out of the room and back down the hallway to the bathroom. We had to do something. As we approached, Halili was coming back out of the bathroom. Niko signaled to me to hit the hallway lights, which I did. Niko charged and began to strike Halili with all his force. He beat Halili severely. We had hoped to not be seen because if we were, it would mean dire consequences for both of us.

In March of 1989, our acts caught up with us, and we were arrested by Sigurimi agents. We were taken into captivity and subjected to all the horrors we had heard about year after year. My head was shaven to embarrass me, and then I was subjected to brutal beatings and phases of various torture. To explain the horrors of torture is to relive it, and for the sake of this book, I will do so but not to its full extent as I am sure that my children will one day eventually read this work. After the head shaving, the beatings, and the interrogations, I was subjected to three distinct phases of torture.

First, I was taken to a cell and had my hands placed in a vise for enhanced interrogation. The interrogators would ask me questions as the vise with a screw wound by them would get tighter and tighter. They would continue to wind the vise until my hands became blue and I screamed from the unbearable pain; the real pain from this event, however, came after your hands were released. My hands would become stiff and harder than rocks. I had the impression that after the event, I would eventually lose my hands. Phase two of my torture came as advanced electroshock therapy. Specially designed metal plates that looked like headphones were placed on my head, and gradual electric current was released through them, provoking shocks and intense pain. This all happened in gradual increments, with the highest setting being so strong that blood would pour from my mouth, ears, and nose. The final phase was the worst. I was brought into a very small cell where the walls were covered in copper netting. My legs were shackled in chains, and a wet carpet was placed underneath my feet. The Sigurimi agent overseeing the whole affair, who was outside the cell as to be protected from the high heat and electric current, would gradually release the electricity while I screamed in pain. He would repeat this exercise and watch the entire affair until I would pass out from the heat and the unbearable pain. I was tortured for days on end for my crimes against the state, but by some miracle from God, I was not killed. I was released from prison broken, in serious pain, but my resolve was never stronger. I returned to AI and began to plan my escape.

Part 4

LAST MEETING WITH MY FATHER

T he last time I saw my father was three months before my brothers and I escaped Albania. I returned to Dedaj from Tirana to meet with my brother so we could plan our journey and ask for our father's blessing together.

My brothers and I had made similar plans before, but we routinely were forced to relinquish them because of fear that Sigurimi agents had been watching us too closely. Regardless of our past failures, we were determined to win, and we collectively refused to give up. We were not raised to be quitters. To us, we saw the little, fat men as merely a small obstacle that we had to overcome to achieve our dreams. I frequently reassured myself of such attitudes. "Don't let those little, fat bastards stand in your way and steal your joy. They hate joy and want everyone to share in their own misery," I would say to myself. Despite all the horrors they subjected us to, I genuinely, at times, felt badly for them. They were completely brainwashed and fooled by the government; they had lost all sense of humanity and lived by a prevailing sense of hatred. They would stop at nothing to hurt social misfits like me and prevent us from achieving any success in our lives; at this point, success meant escape and survival. A loss to them meant death.

After arriving in Dedaj and meeting my brother Paul, we sat to speak with our father. He knew why we had come. The countenance of hope and sadness riddled his entire face. My father began the con-

22

versation by citing a certain saying that remains with me to this day. In fact, he introduced it as an American saying because he had prayed that if we did escape, we would end up there. "The future belongs to the brave, not to cowards. Bravery helps us to overcome any dangers, obstacles, and fears. It enables a person to withstand whatever difficulties may block him from attaining his true goal. One must pay any price for freedom, for one without freedom is a slave. Everyone seeks freedom. Especially in the West, freedom is the highest virtue, and it is sought after by all who are, or consider themselves to be, oppressed. The danger to freedom is always lurking at the corner. Never let your guard down. Don't lose track of the enemy when you are at peace and prosperity. That is when the enemy is most dangerous. If the government offers you something, ask why," he said.

Three days later, after having had many additional discussions with him about America and Western culture, my father gave us his blessing. We said our goodbyes, and he wished us luck, knowing fully well that if our escape was successful, it meant death for some of our family members, most certainly death for him. And that was what happened.

Part 5

THE LAST PLANNING

It was settled. We would attempt to escape on May 29, 1989—a day that could change our lives forever or our lives would be lost forever. The night before, my eldest brother, Tony, arrived in Tirana to spend the night with me at AI. Together, we carefully reviewed the plan we had decided upon; the plan was detailed and elaborate. We were confident but also terrified.

Tony, who at the time was only twenty-five years old, was cooler and more collected than the rest of us. He didn't talk much, but when he did, he commanded the room, and everybody listened. My brother spoke slowly, stuttering a little, but measuring each and every word before he uttered it.

"We will leave Tirana tonight and travel to Shkoder," he said. "We will take the last train from Tirana to Shkoder, this way, this way we will get there in the late, dark of night. This way it is less likely that Sigurimi agents will be following us."

We had prepared to a certain extent to resist the Sigurimi. Over the past few months, we had undergone, in secret, a ton of physical training, but we still were no match for the entire Sigurimi of Albania if they had become aware of our plans.

According to various sources, the Sigurimi was created by the Hoxha communist regime. The Communist Party typically credited the Sigurimi as having been instrumental in their faction's gaining power in Albania over other partisan groups.

The People's Defense Division, formed in 1945 from Hoxha's most reliable resistance fighters, was the precursor to the Sigurimi's five thousand–strong uniformed internal security force.

In the 1980s, the division was organized into five mechanized infantry that could be ordered to quell domestic disturbances posing a threat to the party leadership. By now, the Sigurimi had an estimated ten thousand officers. Approximately 2,500 of whom were assigned to the People's Army.

The organization ceased to exist in name in July 1991 and was replaced by the National Intelligence Service (NIS).

However, many of the officers and leaders of the NIS had served in the Sigurimi, and that the basic structures of the two organizations were similar.

The mission of the Sigurimi was to prevent revolution and to suppress opposition to the regime. The activities of the Sigurimi were directed more toward political and ideological opposition than crimes against persons or property, unless the latter were sufficiently serious and widespread to threaten the regime.

Its activities permeated Albanian society to the extent that every third citizen had either served time in labor camps or been interrogated by Sigurimi officers.

Sigurimi recruits were recommended by loyal party members and subjected to careful political and psychological screening before they were selected to join the service. They had an elite status and enjoyed many privileges designed to maintain their reliability and dedication to the party.

The Sigurimi had a national headquarters and district headquarters in each of Albania's twenty-six districts. It was further organized into sections covering political control, censorship, public records, prison camps, internal security troops, physical security, counterespionage, and foreign intelligence.

The political control section's primary function was monitoring the ideological correctness of party members and other citizens. It was responsible for purging the party, government, military, and its own apparatus of individuals closely associated with the West, especially the United States.

One estimate indicated that at least 170 Communist Party politburo or Central Committee members were executed because of the Sigurimi's investigations. The political control section was also involved in an extensive program of monitoring private telephone conversations.

The Censorship section operated within the press, radio, newspapers, and other communications media as well as within cultural societies, schools, and other organizations.

The physical security section provided guards for important party and government officials and installations.

The counterespionage section was responsible for neutralizing foreign intelligence operations in Albania as well as domestic movements and parties opposed to the Communist Party of Albania.

Finally, the foreign intelligence section maintained personnel abroad and at home to obtain intelligence about foreign capabilities and intentions that affected Albania's national security. Its officers occupied cover positions in Albania's foreign diplomatic missions, trade offices, and cultural centers. Some were even sent abroad, to France and USA, to penetrate the Albanian Diaspora.

The Sigurimi agents were a vicious, heartless, cold, cruel people. They were an extension to the Communist Party arm. As a matter of fact, in my opinion, they were the heart and the soul of the Communist Party because without them, the party could not have survived. They were men from communist families, hard-core communist families. They were mainly Muslims from Central or Southern Albania, but to be fair, there were some Catholics from Mirdita, who had become atheists and joined the Sigurimi. Catholics, who joined the Sigurimi were forced to become atheists because Catholics were not allowed in any branches of government or party roles.

Part 6

ESCAPE

We boarded the train, situated ourselves toward the back, and reviewed the plan one last time. The remainder of trip, we sat in complete silence. Many things rolled through my head during that time; but the images that kept coming back to me were all the faces of the little, fat men in cheap suits in Tirana who had caused me so much trouble. I almost hoped to run into one on my impending journey this night and begin the game of cat and mouse. We were smarter than them tonight, and we were going to win.

We arrived in Shkoder at 10:00 p.m. It was a clear and beautiful night with no clouds visible on the horizon. It was a promising night for our intentions and a night that would live within me for the rest of my life. As we departed the train and walked into the station, our first Sigurimi agent came into view. He was short, ugly and was chewing gum.

How stupid can he be? I thought to myself. Does he know that by chewing gum, he immediately gave himself away to us? At that time, chewing gum was only available to friends and family members of high communist officials. I looked at him, fearing no more. His stupidity gave me confidence.

I walked toward the door and toward him, my blood boiling and my heart pounding, my mind telling me to go over to him and break his neck, but I paused and thought about the overall mission—

escape, freedom. I forced myself to smile at him and walk out the door. As I walked by, his eyes lowered to avoid eye contact with me. He knew that I had recognized him as an agent of the state. As we left, Tony and I split up and began our different routes to the same destination. I turned toward the city square and immediately began to hear footsteps behind me.

I began to walk faster to see if the pace of the steps behind me would try to match my walking speed, which they did; as I slowed, so did theirs. It was clear now. I was definitely being followed, but it was the same game of cat and mouse I had been hoping for. Despite the dangerous nature of the game I was playing, I was enjoying it. The game was high stakes for both of us. Success for me meant freedom, for him, a promotion; failure for both meant almost certain death. The crime of escaping Albania was the highest crime under the communist regime. Betraying the motherland was punishable by death, and Sigurimi agents who failed to stop it faced the same fate. I still wonder what happened to that man.

As I made a right turn onto the piazza, I stooped at the corner, climbed up two steps, and found my way inside a small building and hid behind the door. I watched the agent walk by, confused as to where I disappeared to, and watched him continue up the street. His ineptitude in foot surveillance had worked to my advantage. While I was in the shop, I quickly changed my T-shirt, threw on a blue jacket and a pair of sunglasses, and embarked on the same route as the agent I had just shaken. I followed the road up to the Jordan Misja High School and made a turn down Tom Kola Quarters. Our final destination for this part of our journey was my uncle Rock's house.

Tony had arrived first and was waiting anxiously for me. I knocked on the outside wall door, and he hurried me in. The yard was small, poorly kept, and smelled awful, but it was concealed by eight-foot-high walls, and that was important.

"You look like you have just seen a ghost," he said. I didn't respond and removed the sunglasses from my eyes. "Did anybody follow you?" he asked.

"No," I replied. I followed him into the backyard, and we reviewed the plan again.

The plan called for leaving Shkoder almost immediately. After reviewing everything another time, we were to again split up and meet each other at the bus station where we would embark to Pjetrushan, a village in the highland region. This part of the journey we anticipated would be more dangerous. After all, this was our region, and people in the surrounding cities and villages knew us and our family. Traveling through the city of Koplik, on our direct route, was the most dangerous part because we had a problem with another family, a prominent one with close ties to the communist regime. Members of their family held various roles within the government, Sigurimi, and the local police. Running into one of them could foil all our plans. I was particularly concerned with running into one of the cousins, with whom I had a bad childhood relationship, a local third-shift police officer, who often took this same bus route to his job in Bajze. As the thought of running into him raced through my mind, the bus stopped in Koplik. And there he was, dressed in his police uniform.

He ascended onto the bus, walked past the driver, and skipped the fare payment. He walked with arrogance toward his seat, clearly proud of his role and the benefits that came with his so-called power. At first, he did not see us, but as his eyes panned the bus a second time, his eyes caught mine. Immediately his facial expression changed, and he became visibly uncomfortable; our last meeting ended in a brutal physical altercation between him, myself, and my brother Tony, a fight he did not win. He looked at us, and I didn't know what he thought, but his fear of my brother was apparent. Tony was 6'2", was 220 pounds, had large shoulders, and was fierce. What this police officer didn't know was that we were as uncomfortable as he was. He held our freedom in the balance. His next move determined our outcome. Failure here meant jail or execution and would spoil the plan for two of our other brothers who were waiting for us along various parts of our planned route. Tony had told our brothers very little of our plan. Paul had a big mouth, and Fred was only seventeen years old. We waited in our seats anxiously.

The next stop was Pjetrushan. As the bus slowly approached our destination, Tony and I stood up and proceeded to the rear exit of the bus. We walked back facing the police officer, hearts pounding, minds racing, ready to face our threat if needed; we exited without incident. We got lucky. As the bus left, we breathed a sigh of relief and departed down the road. As we were walking, we inadvertently ran into one of our cousins who was very inquisitive about our trip into his town. After asking too many questions, I began to fear this encounter. My cousin Paul was as nice as anyone, but in a communist country, you cannot trust anybody; the Sigurimi had done too good a job of turning brother against brother, and even father against son. My father always advised us, "Trust no one but each other. Our family will never let you down. But there are no friends in Albania, just many, many spies." As the words of my father rang through my head, I quickly made up some story to get rid of him, and it worked. As Paul walked away, I saw him disappear into the darkness, and I thought to myself what his fate would hold. If he told others of our encounter, the Sigurimi would likely pick him up and interrogate him. His future likely included harsh beatings, torture, accomplice accusations, and potentially death. My heart went out to him. I hoped for his sake and ours that his lips would remain sealed.

Tony and I headed north, walking at a quick pace to meet my brother Paul who was hiding along our route in the woods. Our route took us through rural country, and our journey became eerily quiet. Fear resonated my body, but I did not express it to my brother. We walked in silence along a desolate dirt road—no cars, no people. The night was quiet except for our steps. Finally, Tony pointed me right to a small path that led into the woods. The woods were pitch dark and ominous; the only sound audible was a distant owl and our feet. We continued our trek deep into the woods when finally, we came across a small slope; at the bottom of the ravine was my brother Paul sitting at the foot of a tree.

"What took you so long," he howled at us. We didn't answer. Paul looked tired and thin. I had not seen him in more than six months, but this was not the brother I remembered.

After a minute or so, Tony asked, "Are we ready?" We indicated that we were, and we prayed together to ask for safe passage; we left for Dedaj to retrieve Fred.

We arrived at our childhood home in Dedaj a little later than 1:00 a.m. The house looked warm but lonely. My parents, Prek and Lena, were asleep in one room with the remainder of the family in another. My brother Fred was inside pretending to be asleep. Fred was only seventeen years old and a typical teenager with dreams. He had thought about attending college, but like me, had no interest in attending the Agriculture Institute. He did not want our family's rural life and dreamed of a future in a big city, a future that could never come to fruition in Albania. Fred knew we were coming but was not aware of our plans.

A few nights prior, my brother Tony had spoken to Fred and told him that he would be arriving the night of the twenty-ninth after visiting Tirana but provided no additional details. Tony had instructed Fred to tie a string to his toe and place the end of the string outside the window and leave it there. Upon Tony's arrival, he would notify or wake Fred by tugging at the string. After the tug, Fred was to get up slowly with the lights off to make sure nobody would be woken up, get dressed, and meet Tony outside to do something important. We trusted our parents, and we even had our father's blessing, but we could not let them know we were fleeing that night. We did not want them to worry about the prospect of our death or the prospect of the consequences that were awaiting them if we were successful.

As we approached the house, we could see that everyone was sleeping. We advanced with caution, as to not stir the dog, and waited quietly in the bushes outside the yard. Tony made his way to the window and tugged, while Paul and I watched for spies. The stakes were high, and our fear was prevalent. Surprisingly enough, with all the obstacles placed in front of this night, everything was proceeding according to plan; we were waiting for something to go wrong. Paul and I were prepared to kill. We were not prepared to abandon our plan. After all, killing a Sigurimi agent only meant seven years in prison. Being caught while escaping meant death. Unbeknownst to my brothers, I had a gun with me that I had stolen from a friend in Tirana. It was loaded, and I was ready. As we sat in the bushes waiting, I thought about the prospect of killing another man. I thought about the prospect of using the gun versus using a knife and determined the knife would be better because it wouldn't make a noise. Shortly after, two shadows approached, and I readied my knife. Paul did the same. We sat motionless, barely breathing, awaiting the potential danger that loomed. As the shadows moved closer, the moonlight revealed the faces of my brothers, and I was elated.

When Fred saw us all, he was very confused yet hopeful.

"Are we?" he stated as I placed my hand over his mouth.

I whispered in his ear, "No talking. Too dangerous. Yes, we are."

He looked at me with large eyes, showing his happiness and fear all at the same time. Tony looked over and nodded at us. We collected ourselves and began walking. The next leg of our journey would last for the next seventy-two hours, and it was the most treacherous yet most important in my life. As we reached the edge of our village, realizing that we were alone and without followers, Tony stopped us all and gave us our orders.

"No one talks for the next four hours, no one smokes, no one coughs, no one breathes heavily because the next four villages we pass through will determine our success or failure."

We all understood that Tony was in charge and that he meant what he was saying. We nodded in approval and continued our journey down the connecting dirt road. Emotions high, we refrained from looking back at our family and our home, knowing full well that we would likely never see some members of our family again.

The remainder of the villages we needed to cross through were all connected by this same dirt road. At the entrance of each village was a guard post manned by at least two armed omnipotent men working for the Communist Party. They could stop us from entering the village and hold us until the Sigurimi agents arrived. To be assigned to one of these posts, the guards were screened by the government and agreed to cooperate fully with them; they swore 100 percent allegiance to the government and were equipped with a phone in the post that was connected directly to the regional Sigurimi headquarters in Shkoder. As we were approaching our first post, I spoke to Tony about cutting the visible telephone wires to shut down communications, but Tony had thought it out better than me. In his preparation, he had found a route around the posts. With the first post in sight, we left the road, and three hours later, we had passed our last and final village.

The sun was now rising, and we made a right to start our ascent through the Accursed Mountains (Albanian Alps). A few hundred feet up, we sat and finally turned to face what we hoped would be our past; we said nothing to each other. You could see the sense of nostalgia all over my brothers' faces. I was feeling it too. We did not hate our birthplace. We did not want to leave our family. We hated communism and the government of Albania that was making our lives miserable and punishing us for our last name. Our last glance at the vista below lasted only a few seconds, but it felt like ages. My brothers and I were ready for the next step. Collectively we turned toward our future.

The Accursed Mountains lived up to their namesake. They were tall, rocky, rugged, snow-covered, cold, and what seemed to be endless. As we hiked, I felt as if we were going to be swallowed by them—four small creatures disrupting their majesty. With each step came exhaustion but the promise of freedom; so on we climbed. Hiking in snow is no easy task, so this part of the journey was carefully timed. In the last meeting with my father, he explained to us that if one wishes to walk over the snow without leaving footprints behind, he must wait until the end of May when the snow "boils." Boiling snow is a local term used to describe the melting and freezing process in late spring. The process turns the snow into a thick, dense substance that supports great weight, and thus no impressions are created; but getting to the proper altitude was key. At the base of the mountains, we had to jump from rock to rock to avoid leaving footprints or any indication that we had started the ascent.

There were few ordinary men in the Accursed Mountains, but we knew that there would be plenty of border guards there. Usually, border guards would be sent to their posts there in late April, or so we were told. The first day in the mountains was uneventful. We walked for many hours and took a few breaks as we climbed. We had stored some food for our journey, not much, but enough to get us through. I had secured some boiled eggs and salami, Paul had brought some feta cheese, and Tony had brought some honey; we were forced to ration our meals because we had no idea, at this point, how long our journey to freedom would take. As night approached, we found some sharp, large rocks that connected at their tips to form a cave. Inside the cave, it was cold but dry; it had only one entrance, which could prove problematic if we were cornered, but exhaustion overcame rational thought, and we decided to spend the night. We built a small fire deep within the cave to keep us warm, not visible from the outside, and two of my brothers took shifts guarding the entrance. The night was so dark. One could not see three feet in front of their face outside the cave. Guarding would be difficult, but my brothers Tony and Paul had military experience and were confident in their ability to defend us if necessary. Fred and I were the lucky ones and got much-needed sleep.

The following day, we left the cave early in the morning to continue our ascent. We waited for the sun to rise to gather our bearings and determine our direction. We continued on and headed northwest. Tony had informed the night before that today's expedition would take us close to the border; when we arrived, we would settle somewhere, eat something, and rest for a while before scoping for border guards. We walked on for the next eight hours nonstop before arriving at Tony's target destination. When we arrived, we sat, ate, and rested, all according to plan; Tony left us to scope out the terrain. I watched him climb a large rock and hid behind it, where he stayed for a few hours. He descended toward us, running as fast as he could. Out of breath, he told us he saw guards. He ordered us to stay put and not to move. He advised us to sleep because we were going to wait until late at night to evade the guards. He got up, climbed the rock again, and observed again for a few hours.

When Tony returned, we were all sleeping. He woke us up immediately and informed us of the intel he had gathered. Tony had observed a shift change and determined that the guards worked an eight-hour shift. He had also observed their formation and came to the conclusion that each guard post was roughly five hundred meters from the next and that the guards were not roaming but rather stationary. Based upon the information gathered, Tony assessed that the optimal time for us to proceed would be about 3:00 a.m. in the morning, when the night guards would be sleepy and unresponsive.

We set out at 2:00 a.m. to begin walking; Tony led the pack with Fred, me, and Paul following in linear formation. It was a slow and stealthy walk, testing everything with our feet before fully stepping on it, fearing the area might be land mined to prevent us from escaping. We were also aware from local stories that the area we were crossing was also riddled with sensor wires that sent messages to the guard posts signaling activity in the area. I looked at my brothers and was in awe of their collective courage. I looked forward at Tony, astonished, the master planner of our journey who was fearlessly attempting to lead us to freedom. I looked at Fred and thought of his innocence, unaware of our plans. He was unshaken about the events taking place, keeping cool, calm, collected. I tried to get my mind somewhere else, but I could not get out of my head the image of him being beaten and tortured if we were caught; I worried for him the most. I looked back at Paul, visibly shaken, and he nodded, trying to assure me that we would make it.

As we walked, I thought about many different things, but mostly I thought about death. Not just the possible death of me and my brothers, but also the deaths of so many at the hands of the government. I thought about the possible deaths of the family we were leaving behind and of the metaphoric death of Albania, the real Albania, that came at the hands of communism.

I thought about Sokol Vreshti, a young man from our region who tried to escape to Yugoslavia via Vermosh and failed. Sokol and his companion were outed by a female villager in Vermosh, a city full of spies, and the alarm was sounded. They were caught by the Sigurimi almost immediately, and his companion was shot dead on the spot. He was wounded. The Sigurimi made an example of Sokol; after being wounded, they tied the severed hands of his companion to his and attached them both to the back of a truck. Sokol was dragged behind the truck through town until his death as local villagers looked on and were forced to spit, kick, and taunt him. Most people in Albania would not willingly participate in such behavior, but they had no choice. Not participating could be interpreted or construed as condemnation or worst, sympathy for the traitor, and such action could land you in jail for agitation or propaganda.

I thought about the other brave Albanians who had escaped before us. I thought about all the others who had attempted and failed. I thought about the millions of Albanians, sitting in the secrecy of their homes, who wished that they, too, could escape. I thought of the little, fat men who would lose their jobs because they did not watch me closely enough. This last thought brought a smirk to my face and gave me strength to continue forward.

Finally, I thought of my father and the prayers he led in the secrecy of our home. We prayed a lot as a family, and our father instilled faith as a fundamental aspect of our lives. My father was a strong, wise, and smart man. Speaking very little, he said a lot. Broad, tall, dark, and handsome, with piercing eyes, he commanded the respect of his family, friends, and community. He loved our family with every ounce of his being and gave us the strength and courage to chase our dreams. The thought of leaving him behind brought tears to my eyes. As I was reminiscing, Tony broke my chain of thought.

Tony stopped suddenly and pointed to the right. Paul and I followed his instructions. Tony gave us a thumbs-up indicating that we had successfully broken through the guards' zone and that we were out of danger, at least for the time being. We continued walking for the next three hours until daylight was breaking when we found a place to hide.

"Now we will sleep through the day and walk at night. From this place, the guards can see us during the day," Tony said.

As we began to rest, Tony left again to study the upcoming terrain. When Tony returned, he had gathered enough info for us to make the next move. He informed us that he believed that we were close to the border with Yugoslavia and that there was not a second guard line that we would have to pass. At night, we began to walk again. This night was the darkest night of them all, and the terrain was absolutely treacherous; after just a few minutes, we decided to abandon our plans because we feared falling from the steep cliffs. We would have to risk walking in the daylight if we wanted to continue. We returned to our hideout and determined our next steps.

The following day would be the final day of our journey. Tony woke us just before dawn, and we started walking. Tony instructed us to make a left turn between two mountain peaks, but something seemed wrong. I never liked making left turns. Lefts scared me. Lefts would take us east, and we needed to head west. We had veered off our original and planned course. I had no choice but to trust my brother. After all, he had taken us this far already. After a few hours, my fears came to fruition, and we became terribly lost, lost so badly that we actually contemplated giving up and turning around. But God had other plans for us. He presented us with a solution.

At this point, we had been heading east for nearly six hours, far off our original charted course, when all of a sudden, we heard a loud and distinct noise—tree or wood chopping. We had gone too far east, and there was most likely an Albanian in the area, and we were in danger of being caught. We had to investigate and determine the nature of our threat; we couldn't let them sound the alarm for the Sigurimi. Tony charged Paul and me with the task while he and Fred stayed behind. As we approached the noise, we came across exactly what we had anticipated—a man chopping wood and clearing brush. Old, tired, beaten, and broken, it did not look like he would pose a serious threat. He was alone, accompanied only by a tattered backpack hanging from a tree that likely contained his lunch. He stopped for a minute.

Was he tired? Or did he notice us? I wondered. I grabbed my revolver, stood ready, perched down, and waited. I did not want to kill him. I assumed he had a family, and I thought about his wife and children. He picked up his ax and began chopping again. We moved in closer. At this moment, he saw us, stopped, and looked perplexed with fear radiating in his deep eyes.

He saw my revolver and stared at it; a piece of cold metal that could kill him and end everything he knew. He shivered in fear. He finally gathered enough strength to ask, "Who are you? What do you want?"

We didn't reply. He begged us not to kill him, telling us about his wife and children at home. He bargained with us, telling us that he would deny seeing us and that he would not share our encounter with anyone as long as we spared his life. Finally, Paul spoke.

"We are trying to get to Dukagjin," he said. "Which way to Dukagjin? This way?" Pointing east. "Or that way?" Pointing west.

Through a broken voice, the man responded that walking west would take us to Montenegro and walking east would take us to Dukagjin. He explained that if we were to continue along very fast, we would reach Montenegro (then part of Yugoslavia) in forty-five minutes and that there were no border guards there right now. The guards were at Tropoje Post. He insisted that he was telling the truth and that he was not a government spy, and then he pleaded for his life again. As I held my gun to the man's head, Paul tied him to a tree loosely with a small rope that we had brought with us. We assured him that death would not come from our hands but that we needed assurance that he would not run to the village and call the alarm. He was still scared but thankful for the outcome. We left to return to our brothers as fast as we could, knowing fully well that when this man broke free, he would betray us and our compassion.

We met Tony and Fred shortly after and informed them of recent events. They agreed with our assessment and we began a mad dash to Montenegro. Walking fast, half running, I followed my brothers Tony and Fred up the mountain, but Paul was falling behind. Paul stopped. He was exhausted, but there was no time to waste; the mountain was steep and bare, and we were clearly visible to anyone who was looking. I turned back for Paul, grabbing his arm and dragging him up the incline. Tony came to my aid. With our brother in hand, we saw the man whom we had tied up, running down the ravine. We knew exactly what he was doing. He was calling the alarm because he had to. Failure to report us could cost him his life.

As we approached the pyramid, the erection that separated Montenegro from Albania, I could read the abbreviation for Yugoslavia, and I could almost taste freedom. We pulled Paul harder; uncooperative, he begged us to leave him behind, a sacrifice to guarantee our safety. We didn't comply. We were all making it to freedom or nobody was. We would drag Paul the rest of the way if we had to. The alarm sounded. The border guards, armed with heavy machine guns, were in pursuit and running up the mountain. We were tired, weak, disheveled, and hungry, and they were closing in. After making it this far, we were determined to win. By the grace of God, we were able to muster our last ounce of strength to carry Paul. As Tony lifted his left arm and I, his right, the guards began shooting.

A barrage of bullets was unleashed, and the terrifying sound cracked through the thin mountain air. As the bullets whizzed by, I thought again of the oppression my family had suffered, the tortures I had endured, the depression of my people, and the promise of a new life. I mixture of hope and enragement came over me and quickened my pace. We were fighting a battle of good versus evil, and we were close to crossing the border. With only a few yards remaining, the intensity of the fire weakened. When we touched the pyramid, it stopped. Freedom had beaten oppression. Good had conquered evil. The promise of our future dreams had triumphed the misery of our past. Life had prevailed over death.

Freedom was beautiful. The sun was shining. The air was fresh, and the smell of promise percolated through the air. The feeling was almost indescribable for anyone not familiar with life under tyranny; I had waited my whole life for this feeling, and here it was for the first time. I had accomplished the first part of my journey, but we still had a long way to go to reach the United States.

From the top of the mountain, we could see parts of Montenegro that appeared populated, and we were overjoyed that we were so close. We wasted little time in continuing on; we placed our jackets underneath our buttocks and began sliding down toward the town of Vuthaj. We slid down the mountain for hours, all four brothers, and we felt like children. At this point, we knew we were safe from imminent danger, but we still proceeded with caution. After all, we were still teetering on the mountain cliffs in high altitude. After a while, it became apparent that we would not make Vuthaj before nightfall, so we stopped to build a fire, find a hideout, and spend one more night in the mountains; this would be our final night in hiding. The following morning, we would surrender ourselves to the Yugoslav forces.

The Yugoslav guards were young men, nicely dressed, well-spoken, and nonthreatening. They spoke to us as equals and made us feel at ease. They assured us that we were safe now and provided us the first real meal that we had in days. Most of the soldiers were my age, but our differences were stark. It was clear that life was much different and much better just beyond the majesty of the mountains. As we sat and ate, two civilians approached us; one spoke Albanian, and the other did not. The Albanian-speaking gentleman was in his late forties and was dressed very well; his appearance convinced me that he held a prominent role within the Yugoslav hierarchy. He introduced himself as Novi, an agent with the Ministry of Interior Affairs of the Socialist Republic of Yugoslavia. Novi was an ethnic Albanian.

Novi and his partner took us to a small town in Montenegro called Plav to board us for the night and to feed us dinner; the next day, he would interview us to understand our reasons for escaping. After several interviews and hours of interrogation by the Yugoslav security forces, we were taken before a judge who sentenced us to thirty days in jail for illegally crossing the border into Yugoslavia. After our sentence, we were to be transported to a refugee camp in Belgrade.

Part 7

THE INTERNMENT OF THE FAMILY

The following account is taken and compiled from stories provided to me by my family who experienced this firsthand.

At 5:00 a.m. on a hot and sticky day in June, my parents' house was surrounded by old soviet-made military vehicles. Sigurimi agents, police officers, and military personnel stormed my home and ordered my family to the ground. As the fat, little men walked around our modest house, they began counting all the family members to make sure that the nine members of the family still living there were all accounted for; they were ordered to remain on the floor and await further instructions.

My mother, terrified, scared, and trembling, began to cry—not tears of fear or sorrow but rather tears of joy. This intrusion into her home was her first indication that we were alive and our journey had been successful, but it was not their first interaction with the government since our escape. Days earlier, government agents arrived in Dedaj to notify my parents that all four of their sons had been executed for betraying the motherland, and they were heartbroken. This new intrusion was different from the last. This was the beginning stages of punishment, and my mother knew what that meant. She knew that we were successful. Roughly 12,500 families were interned in Albania during this time, according to official reports, but many people believe the actual number to be much higher.

My family was ordered to march outside one by one and get into the back of the trucks. As they got into formation, the agents readied their weapons and pointed them at my family; my father walked out first. As the remainder of my family piled into the trucks on the street, a crowd of villagers began to gather to watch the encounter. The villagers knew what was happening. As odd as this sounds, these types of events were all too common in Albania; the villagers came to stand in solitude with my family and to say goodbye. They knew that when a family is interned, there is a great possibility that those people would never be seen or heard from again. Internment camps were forever, and their whereabouts were completely unknown to all outside the high circles of the Communist Party.

As the crowd grew larger and larger, many of the officials on-site became visibly nervous. The villagers were irate at the proceedings and started to become unruly. This was an attack on one of their own, in an area of already deep-rooted communist resentment. The crowd was fearless, indomitable, and was ready to strike to save their relatives from the coercion of the government. The people in Northern Albania were disappointed with the regime, and tensions were high; people were not willing to be fooled any longer. The sun was fading on communism quickly. The clans assembled had come to the Lumaj family's aid before, and our ties with the surrounding clans, most often relatives, was strong. The soldiers knew this and called for backup.

> The Lumajes (who were also known as Sokoli) had endured a lot of the course of their history in Albania. My clan, hugely nationalistic and pugnacious, fought the Turks, the Serbs, and the Communists—each and every time they threatened our family's way of life. In 1909, the Turks attacked the Lumaj compound because members of my family raised the Albania flag, a risky action at the time, to signal their opposition to the Ottoman Empire. It was in the dark of Christmas night when the Turks first attacked

the Lumaj compound. The brutal, surprise cannon attack originated from a place called Zabele; fearing the resiliency of the Lumaj forces and the strength of the fortress walls, the Ottoman Empire set out first to obliterate the compound walls and set fire the to the homes—forcing the men, women, and children out for slaughter.

As the Turkish forces besieged the compound in Dedaj with cannon fire, the parishioners attending Christmas Mass fled out of the church and started to take up arms. My grandfather Mark, his brothers, and other male relatives had prepared for this attack. They were aware that the Turks were preparing to attack them. A few days before, they had seen three military garrisons gather in Zabele, which situated on higher ground than our compound, and immediately became aware of the seriousness of the attack coming—higher ground would mean that the Turkish attack would be effective. As the Turkish garrisons gathered there, Mark, my grandfather and the patriarch of the Lumaj clan at the time, ordered all the women and children out of the compound and sent them to a safe place. As the family left the compound to travel to the safe area, the Albanian flag was raised even higher, infuriating the Turks even more.

This was a time of great confrontation and chaos in Albania; Albanian Catholics in the North were fighting to become independent from the Turkish Muslims, and my family led this fight.

Unbeknownst to the Turks who were attacking my family's compound, the Malesors, villagers from the district of Malesi e Madhe, had been notified of the impending attack on the Lumajes. Men of fighting age from all over Malesi e Madhe

(Shkrel, Hot, Kelemed, Grude, and Kastart) went to church in Shkrel that night armed to the teeth. They were ready to join fighting the Turks if they dared to attack the Lumajes. An attack on the Lumajes was viewed as an attack on every man from Malesi e Madhe; it was an attack on their national identity, an attack on their flag, and an attack on the leaders of their independence movement. If the Lumajes were under siege, they would do all that they could collectively to drive the Ottoman Empire out of their land.

As the Turks pounded the Lumaj's compound, my grandfather led his forces quietly out of the church and around the mountain. The Lumaj forces marched up the mountain and positioned themselves behind the Turks and on higher land. My grandfather and his forces attacked from behind. Enemy forces were caught by surprise and were slaughtered by my grandfather's men. The Turks withdrew and ran, losing this battle, but not the war.

The following day, additional Ottoman forces arrived in Dedaj to wipe out the Lumaj clan, but to no avail. By the time they arrived, the entire Lumaj clan had left for Croatia, where they were forced to stay in exile for three years. Frustrated by their lack of success, the Turks burned the remainder of the Lumaj compound to the ground.

My grandfather and his brother returned to Albania many times secretly to lead various attacks on the Turks until 1912, when they finally defeated them once and for all. During these attacks, my grandfather lost his brother, Nikoll Sokoli.

Though the Turks had been defeated and had left the region, the persecution of my family continued. As the Turks left, communism rose, and it became an even more severe enemy to my family and to our country.

In 1939, the communist evil began to establish its bad seed in Albania. The Lumajes decided to fight them as well. They were a godless, vicious, dictatorial, malevolent force that would rule Albania with an iron fist until 1991.

In 1944 to 1945, hundreds of communist partisans targeted members of my family and killed many Lumajes. During the brutal battles between the Northern Albanian allies and the Communists, the Communists slayed Gjon Mirashi, Pjeter Kola, Zef Mirashi, Prek Leka, and his brother—all members of my family. The Communists were ultimately successful and retaliated harshly. They burned our houses; confiscated our property, our lands, and our livestock; and terrorized the Malesi e Madhe region for not submitting to the communist regime rule. This time was known as the Uprising of Malesi e Madhe.

My father, realizing the anxiousness of the crowd, made an appeal for serenity. He signaled to the elders assembled that he didn't want bloodshed and that he feared an eventual and brutal retribution.

"They are doing their job!" he yelled. "Do not attack them. They do not know any better, and their day will come. Right now, we are not any match for them, at least not yet! They have all the weapons. They disarmed us. They promised to protect us, but now they persecute us. Still do not attack. Their day will come." As the final words left my father's mouth, the soldiers and agents of the government began to beat him and the other members of the family and threw them down in the trucks. The convoy began and proceeded to the middle of the village where other soldiers had placed the remaining villagers to witness my family being dragged off to face their punishment. They were instructed to spit and hit them as the procession moved past. Much to the dismay of the government, almost no one in Dedaj participated.

Part 8

FAMILY LIFE IN A CONCENTRATION CAMP

After having been driven for hours on end, my family arrived in a small village south of the city of Shkoder. My family was removed from the convoy and placed with other political prisoners being interned for various different crimes against the government. The entire family was placed in a small barracks—a single concrete room with a few wooden benches, which I was told was unbearably hot in the summer and excruciatingly cold during the winter. The camp was surrounded by a tall barbed wire fence and was supervised by armed guards twenty-four hours a day, seven days a week. All internees were subjected to harsh physical labor to pay for their crimes or the crimes of their family members; a typical day would last at least twelve hours, and there was no remuneration. Food was provided, but it was scarce, and the quality was poor. Men were typically beaten or tortured for noncompliance or performing too little work in the eyes of the supervisory agent; women were often subjected to rape, which was a typical punishment used to humiliate noncommunist families. My father died a few years later while being imprisoned and worked to death. He made a final plea to my mother on his deathbed, asking her and the family to forgive their captors and the government for all the terrible crimes they had committed against my family.

Here is an account from Shannon Woodcock's Against a Wall:

Most men and women who were arrested and convicted of political crimes (as opposed to ordinary crimes) had not committed the crimes of which they were accused. The state routinely fabricated absurd accusations against individuals as a way to maintain high levels of fear—of enemy attack and of sudden denunciation—in the community. Groups liable to attract persecution included families that had been Democrats, intellectuals, or landowners before the communist period; families of those who had left for foreign countries; ethnic minorities such as Greeks and Vlach Albanians; and those who had simply been accused of dissent against the regime. Different groups were targeted during the various phases of Albanian politics, and those persecuted always included women.

After Hoxha split with the USSR and its allies in 1961, for example, the Russian wives of Albanians were arrested as foreign spies and imprisoned. During the Cultural and Ideological Revolution of the 1970s, the Party of Labor worked to emancipate women from having the sole responsibility for housework and from organized marriages. Both moves were driven by political agendas rather than being primarily about the party's concern for young women. Women were denounced for wearing cosmopolitan clothes such as short skirts and for associating with foreign men such as Kosovar Albanians or the sailors who arrived on ships in Durres. In the late 1970s and early 1980s, purges of the communist politburo and elite increased, which led to the persecution of the wives and families of the purged communist ministers.

The Albanian state followed Soviet tradition. It accused individuals or groups of fabricated political crimes, arrested and interrogated the accused until they confessed or refused to confess—and often wrote the confessions themselves. They held many trials in public buildings equipped with loud speakers so the broadcasted proceedings would educate and intimidate the population. Women were accused of the same kinds of political crimes as men, of which sabotage and espionage (Art. 47 in the 1977 Constitution), and agitation and propaganda (Art. 55) were punished with up to ten years in prison.

A friend's family had fled Albania in the late 1940s, becoming refugees in Italy and then citizens in Australia. They returned to Albania in the 1960s, when Albanian spies approached Albanian refugees and deceptively offered them the right of return without punishment. Many Albanians returned at this time, only to be arrested as enemies of the people when they arrived back in Albania. After returning in this way, they lived under surveillance, many in prisons and labor camps. My friend's brother, then aged sixteen, was immediately imprisoned in the labor camp prison of Burrel upon return. He was later sent to the notorious psychiatric hospital of Elbasan, where he died. My friend lived her everyday life known as an enemy of the people for her bad biography (the terms used by both state and society), knowing that colleagues who worked with her at the isolated factory in the north of Albania informed on all her movements to the party. She could not imagine that revolution or political change was possible; she kept silent and tried to fit in as best she could.

On the morning of her arrest, which had not been preceded by any unusual events or problems, she was taken to a building in the local regional city and shown into a concrete cell that had neither a window nor a bed. For the next seven months, she was deprived of sleep, kept hungry, cold and alone, and beaten in daily interrogations. She was asked to confess to a range of crimes that she had not commit. She saw the sky just once each day as she was taken to the bathrooms along a corridor that had an iron roof and chain walls. The guards watched her every move, including in the bathroom. She still does not know what the drug was they gave her that made her bleed nonstop as if heavily menstruating for the entire seven months. The guards did not provide her with rags for the blood, and in interrogations, they consistently referred to her as miscarrying a bastard child. Sex outside marriage in Albania was so severely frowned on at that time that to accuse a young, unmarried Albanian woman of pregnancy interpellated her as, in my friend's words, a slut, forever totally outside social boundaries of honorable interaction.

My friend was weak from the constant blood loss, hunger, and exhaustion; she understood that the guards could rape her at any time. Rape was considered the worst event possible for a woman. The shame of rape accrues to the victim and her family, not to the rapist. My friend often reflects even now that the fear of rape was more powerful than the actuality of rape would have been, and she knows that her torturers' aim was to treat her as an already dishonored sexual object.

After seven months, she signed the thick pages of her pre-prepared confession. She still doesn't know what exactly was in those pages as the accusations were many, varied, and untrue, and they now are muddied in her memory by exhaustion and pain. She does remember seeing her confession as a failure of will at the time. On the basis of it, she was convicted of agitation and propaganda and sentenced to ten years prison. In 1978, at the age of thirty-one, she was transported in the back of a prison truck to the women's prison at Kosovë të Elbasan. It was just a few months after the female prisoners who had built the prison had finished the construction and been moved in as the first inmates.

This is according to Fatjona Mejdini, BIRN, Tirana.

Rumors that women from families persecuted by the communist authorities were raped as a punishment have circulated over the past two decades, but a genuine public debate only erupted recently after the issue was highlighted by former Albanian singer and author Alida Hisku, now living in Germany.

In a newspaper interview, Hisku admitted that she was raped by a prosecutor while she was held in custody.

Although she then withdrew the comments, they sparked widespread debate.

Simon Mirakaj, the former director of the Albanian Institute of Formerly Persecuted People—a former political prisoner himself— told BIRN that the phenomenon of rape under communism was widespread especially when families of enemies of the party were detained.

"Members of the old secret police, the Sigurimi, would pick up the most beautiful wives of the prisoners. Nobody could say a word about this otherwise they would be killed," he said.

Mirakaj said that there are dozens of other women with stories like Hisku, but it is very difficult for them to openly admit what happened.

Agim Musta, a researcher and author who spent eleven years in communist prisons, also told BIRN that the phenomenon was widespread, but "don't expect that any of those abused women is going to speak openly about that."

"We live in a conservative society in which speaking about rape openly is very difficult, bearing in mind the fact that those women now are in their later years," he said.

Musta said that during the interviews that he did about the varieties of persecutions under communism, it emerged that the worst years for such abuses were between 1945 and 1950.

"Horrible things happened with dissident women or the wives of political prisoners during that time in prison and everywhere else. Later, the party became centralized, and officials and Sigurimi people were afraid that somebody would spy on them and started to do it in a more secret way," he said.

Agron Tufa, an author and the director of the Institute for Communist Crimes, told BIRN that the real reason why this issue was not discussed openly before relates to the poor state of media in the country.

"What kind of security will those women have to speak out if they see that the Albanian media is full of the opinions and interviews of people who were part of the old secret police," Tufa said.

He said that there was no more cause for skepticism about the use of rape as punishment under communism because people who have lived through that time and others who have had access to secret files confirm that it was widespread.

Tufa believes that now is the time for the state to encourage the victims to come forward and for the abusers to be punished.

At least 450 Albanian women were executed under communism, and thousands were kept in detention camps and used as forced labor.

Part 9

My Life in a Refugee Camp

T he camp we were placed in was situated in an area called Camp Trim in Northeastern Belgrade. The camp itself was actually quite large and consisted of several small hotels and huts; my brothers and I were given two adjoining rooms in one of the hotels for the length of our stay. The conditions were not ideal, but the United Nations was trying its best to make us comfortable, and it was a huge upgrade from what we had recently experienced back home. The camp was a melting pot of all different races and religions, and our backgrounds were all very different. But we shared a common dream, an eventual journey to America and the embrace of true and actual freedom. At night, we would often gather to tell stories and share our dreams; we would talk about the horrors we suffered under communism or tyranny, the people back home still facing it, and what we wanted to do when we reached our envisioned destination. We would talk about the endless possibilities that awaited us in America and the promise of freedom.

People should know that freedom is the exception to the rule. If you were to read almost any book accounting the human experience since biblical times, you would quickly come to the conclusion that most people, at one point or another, were forced to live under fear, oppression, and the servitude of tyranny. But during my time in the camp, it was becoming clear that the world was changing and changing rapidly. Eastern Europe was collapsing; Reagan, Thatcher, and Pope John Paul II had taken strong stands against communism, and they were working tirelessly to liberate Eastern Europe and root out the horrors of the regimes standing there.

My time at the camp gave me the opportunity to learn a lot about Western values and the importance of Judeo-Christian traditions encompassed within those values. I used my time to reflect on the meaning of freedom and various figures throughout history whose sacrifices changed the world by accepting and embracing the challenges and burdens of their time. I thought to myself, What if Jesus Christ had not accepted the cross? Would the world be the same? What if the founders of the United States had refused the responsibility of fighting back against British tyranny and establishing the greatest nation on earth? What if Lincoln lacked the courage to free the slaves? What if Reagan, Thatcher, and the pope had refused to stare down communism and fight for human rights? The world would not have been the same.

Though I was elated to live in freedom, it was also very dangerous to reside in one of these camps. At that time, agents from the Ministry of Interior Affairs of Yugoslavia, called UDB, were working directly with the KGB, the Russian spying agency. The Russians and the Serbs were closely connected; the Serbs were actively engaged in fighting the Kosovar Muslims, and the Russians were fighting the Americans and the Chechens—both groups needed bodies to accomplish their goals, and with the promise of rewards, refugees were easy recruits. The camp was full of agents from both groups, and they were offering anything and everything to attract new recruits—free weapons training, combat training, language classes, and the promise of good money for those who signed on. We could clearly identify the refugees who made the mistake of working for the UDB or KGB. They would often disappear for weeks on end and then suddenly return. These refugees never experienced the freedom that enticed them to leave their homelands in the first place. Selling their souls for the promise of quick rewards blacklisted many of them from moving on and being resettled. They were forced to stay in Yugoslavia.

Shortly after entering Yugoslavia, we had our first encounter with the UDB while serving our sentence in jail. The agents that approached us called us into a small interrogation room one by one and spoke to us in Albanian. The agents name sounded Serbian, but he looked to me like an ethnic Albanian. He was in his early fifties, in great physical shape, and had very sharp eyes. He promised me the world. He offered me housing, a steady job, schooling, cash incentives, and settlement in Kosovo if I agreed to work with them and spy on their behalf. My brothers and I all refused, and much to our surprise, they left us alone for a while.

The CIA was also present in these camps, whether they admit to it or not, but at a much more surreptitious level. We heard rumors of these men infiltrating the camp at night and speaking to refugees who were East Germans, Russian, and even some Albanians. One day, one of these men approached me while I was out jogging a few miles from my hotel at camp. As I was jogging, a black Mercedes-Benz pulled next to me, then a man rolled down the window and called my name. The gentleman spoke English (which I didn't know) and Serbo-Croatian (which I had just learned). He asked me to join him for a drink in Old Belgrade at a bar called Dragovic Restaurant and Bar, at Carice Milice 7, Belgrade, Serbia. He handed me a business card with the appropriate information and asked me to take a trolley to the location to meet him. Intrigued, I decided to attend.

Later that evening, I took the trolley to the restaurant to see what all the fuss was about. I was greeted at the door by a gentleman in his midthirties who addressed me in Serbo-Croatian and who walked me to a private back room in the restaurant to meet with the American. As I walked into the room, I was greeted by the man from the car and a beautiful female companion sitting next to him with a hello in Albanian; the doorman left quickly. He introduced himself as John, and she introduced herself as Vera Vretic. Vera spoke both perfect English and Albanian. As our conversation began, it became quite clear that John knew a lot about me and my family. He informed me that my family had been taken to a concentration camp and that their internment had started a few days after we had crossed the border. It was an interesting meeting to say the least.

As I left the meeting, I decided to reflect on my conversation with John and Vera and made the decision to walk back to the camp versus take the trolley. I made the wrong decision. Just after 11:30 p.m., I was close to my hotel, maybe a hundred meters away, when two agents of the UDB stopped me in the street and ordered me to provide them with my ID card, which we were required to carry to freely move about the city. After confirming who I was, the agents threw me into their car and sped off. We traveled for forty-five minutes to the outskirts of the city down a road I had not traveled before; nobody in the car spoke the entire drive. When we arrived at their destination, we came to a gate in which the two men I was driving with presented credentials to two guards providing the property's security; they opened the gate, and we went inside. They parked the car, ordered me to get out in Serbian, and walked me to a creepy, dark, and cold stand-alone building in the middle of the yard. We went inside and proceeded down a long, dark corridor with many doors, all of which were closed. Finally, I was taken into one of these rooms where another man was inside and waiting. The room had three chairs, one table, and an odd reclining chair covered in belt straps and wires. As I stood there taking inventory, I noticed my escorts gave the appropriate salutations to their commanding officer, and I realized I was with someone important; I didn't know why I was there, but I would soon find out.

The man sitting signaled me to sit down and offered me a cigarette; he asked the other two men to leave. After pleasantries were exchanged and our cigarettes extinguished, my interrogation began. At first, he eased into it, asking me questions about my recent meeting with the Americans, my association with them, my reasons for the meeting, and if I had planned to meet with them again. I kept my responses curt and truthful; but he did not believe my story. The pressure intensified, and he began to strike me across the face; my nose immediately burst open, and my boiling blood started to flow. He screamed at me, yelled about my lies, and called the other two men back inside. They grabbed me. We struggled but I was overcome and placed on the reclining chair and strapped in. I was terrified that this was an electric chair, and I thought about death.

They tilted the chair down and blindfolded me by placing a towel over my face. They began to pour large buckets of water over my face, and it went down my throat and nose, preventing me from breathing; the interrogation continued. Now, all three were screaming at me about my meeting with the Americans. My answers didn't change, and they repeated this exercise on me four additional times. After realizing I had no new information to provide, they untied me and sent me into another room at gunpoint. This room was pitch-black and had no windows and no lights; they pushed me inside. After about a minute of listening to them argue in Serbo-Croatian, they began to punch and kick my body all over. I could not see anything and had no idea where my captors' blows were coming from. They beat me so severely that I soon lost consciousness.

The next thing I remember was waking up in a local hospital covered in blood a few days later. I was covered in cuts and black-and-blue marks from head to toe. I was in great pain, but relatively speaking, this was an easy interrogation compared to the ones I had suffered at the hands of the Sigurimi in Albania. The UDB wanted me to choose Yugoslavia over America. Their efforts were in vain. I was not fleeing one tyranny to come to another. A few weeks later, I attended an interview process with my brothers at the United States Embassy in Belgrade. There, I met John again. He was the person they put in charge of the refugee screening process, and his decision would determine our eligibility to enter the United States. As I sat there, I watched him review my application intensely. As he came to the end of my application, he asked me only one simple question. Why did I choose the United States three times in the section where it asked me to rank my relocation choices? Why hadn't I chosen a second or third choice? I told him firmly that we had left Albania with the intent of becoming Americans and that we didn't want to go anywhere else.

John smiled, knowing the misery we had suffered thus far to get to this point, and said simply, "Welcome to America."

Part 10

PREPARING FOR THE USA

A ny potential refugee who wished to come to the United States had to go through a process in which the government determined you to be "clean." Clean meant passing a background check, going through an intense medical examination, and pledging allegiance to our new adoptive country. We were happy to do it; we wanted to be Americans, learn the language, and embrace the Judeo-Christian values of America's founding. Going to America is the dream of millions around the world, and we were the few lucky ones getting an opportunity to come. Waiting nine months in a refugee camp and going through this process was well worth it. America is a beacon of hope to all, and legal immigration makes our nation stronger; it is a place where people all over the world, regardless of their background, can come to search for freedom and escape the political, ethnic, and religious oppressions or persecutions of their governments.

Illegal immigration is an insult to the sacrifices made by the refugees who made the decision to come here legally and take part in the proper processes. Instead of respecting America's laws, illegal immigrants are blatantly breaking them and coming here with a sense of entitlement; this problem is becoming more evident with each new wave of immigrants, and it is getting out of hand. Nowadays, illegals refuse to learn the language, refuse to submit to proper screening, and have no intent on ever acclimating into American society. Worst of all, these immigrants, now, actively resist American culture and try to impose their own upon the American people. I never understood the mentality of these people; how could anyone who comes here, searching for freedom and opportunity, want to bring the same policies and practices with them that they just fled. My, how the times have changed. Immigration is no longer about freedom. It's about benefits, and that's the problem.

Part II

ENCOUNTERING LIBERALISM AND GOVERNMENT DEPENDENCY IN THE UNITED STATES

I never thought I would find socialism in the United States. I was wrong. In January 1990, my brothers and I landed at JFK International Airport in New York City to begin our new life. After landing, we were processed for roughly three hours before being allowed to leave the airport. During our processing, the immigration authorities brought us a translator to help facilitate our communication, and we were shocked at the information they provided us. During the course of our conversation, the translator brought in some forms and encouraged us to apply for government aid, which she called public assistance. Dumbfounded, my eldest brother Tony inquired further and found out, from the translator, that because of our status, we qualified for welfare programs that would help pay for rent and food if we wanted assistance. To her shock, my brother raised his voice and sternly said, "No, we did not come here to live on government handouts," Tony stated. An odd look portrayed across the woman's face, and Tony continued, "We came here for the American dream and for American freedom. We do not believe the government can help us. We ran from intrusive government and are not interested. But thank you anyway." Nowadays, airports all around the world encourage people to come to America for the aid we provide immigrants. Much to their demise, many take it immediately and are stuck in government servitude for the remainder of their lives.

From New York, we embarked on a flight to Michigan that same night, where a distant relative had offered to take us in until we got settled. On the flight, I reminisced about Albania and the family members we had left behind. Albania was a small country with just over three million people, and it had been turned into a hellhole; after our escape, I had done some research and found out that my family had become part of the 10 percent of all families being imprisoned by the government in one of twenty-two political prisons throughout the country. I worried for them. I was sad knowing the misery they were experiencing, undergoing many of the tortures myself, and I felt guilty. I was bothered, knowing the strong will of my father and other members of the family, that if they if they did not comply with the government's demands, that they would be shot and buried in a mass, unmarked grave for political prisoners, and that their eventual fate would be unknown to us. Currently the Association of Politically Persecuted People in Albania confirms a single burial place of over four thousand bodies discovered during the regime of Enver Hoxha, but the total number still remains a mystery.

A few hours later, we landed in Michigan. As we approached the tarmac to land, we could see the lights of Detroit and large snowflakes falling from the sky. Michigan was cold, frigid cold, a cold we hadn't experienced since our time in the mountains. Once we walked out of the airport, we met a man named Joe Lulaj, our distant cousin, who was waiting to pick us up. Like us, Joe was an Albanian escapee who had escaped with most of his family a few years earlier. He didn't know us, and we didn't know him, but we shared a bond. He helped us to his car and drove us through the ice and snow for two hours before reaching his house in Sterling Heights, Michigan, where he lived with his parents and siblings. His father, Nikoll Lulaj, was in his seventies and very tall; when we walked through the door, he stood up, wrapped his arms around us, and began to weep. He informed us that he was good friends with our father and that he was praying for his and our family members who were left behind; he had family in internment camps too.

A few days later, the Lulajes invited us to attend Catholic Mass with them at a local Albanian American church; there are a lot of Albanians in Michigan. We had been praying Catholics all our lives, but organized religion was unfamiliar to us because it was outlawed in Albania, and the government had done everything it could to keep it out of mainstream life. Churches were closed, burned to the ground, and most of our priests had been executed by government agents. We enjoyed mass and even were announced by the priest at the end of the service. The priest made an appeal to the congregation to help us with jobs and financial assistance and announced where we were staying. To our astonishment, we were accepted with arms wide open, and people began donating to us on the spot. People came over with money, clothing, and needed household items all to get us settled; the generosity of strangers was amazing, and it's a happy memory I will always hold dear to my heart. Within a few weeks, job offers were made, and we had raised enough money to go out on our own. We rented a small apartment, bought a car, and we were all working.

I began working for Pete Shkreli, an Albanian American whose father had left Albania many years ago. Pete owned a local Burger King and employed us all as fry cooks and dining staff. Unbeknownst to me, we were related, and he came from a powerful Catholic family in Northern Albania full of anti-communist dissidents. Pete was born in Italy, and his parents were still there waiting to come to the United States to join him and his family. Many members of Pete's family were also imprisoned in political prisons in Albania. Pete's family helped shape my thoughts on the American political system, and when his father joined him in America, we became very close. Pete's father often tied American liberalism to communism, and his assessment made sense to me. "Liberals have no identity," he would often say, "they don't embrace a national identity, a religious identity, a political identity, a racial identity. Liberals have no identity at all. Liberal ideology supersedes everything else in their minds. They fear manhood, independence, prosperity, religious values, property, and individuality. Their mentality is communist. They've just renamed it to fool the public." He despised liberalism and communism equally; he became a staunch Republican and was a great man.

After living in Michigan for about six months, one of Pete's cousins, Zef, came to visit us at our apartment. He lived in New York City and spoke of the endless opportunities that awaited there if one was willing to work hard and ingrain themselves in the local Albanian community. He convinced us to consider moving. After a few weeks, we decided to go to New York. We settled in the Morris Park section of the Bronx, an old Italian-American neighborhood riddled with Albanians from Montenegro. The Albanians from Montenegro are an interesting bunch; they speak Serbo-Croatian better than Albanians, and their names end in vic, indicating that they are more ingrained in Serbian culture more so than Albanian. They did not like us at all and were closely tied to the Kosovar community that was supportive of the communist regime in Albania.

The Albanians from Montenegro were the established group in New York City at the time, so assimilating with them became important for our success in the community; later on, Northern Albanians would also become a dominant ethnic group in the Bronx. To assimilate, we started attending their Catholic Church on Park Avenue in the Bronx, and tensions quickly faded. Though we did have to listen to mass in an archaic Albanian dialect that was unfamiliar to us. Zef and his brothers Mark, Peter, and Nosh were tremendously helpful in making our transition easy and smooth; they helped us find jobs and enrolled us in English as a Second Language courses. My brothers found various jobs in the Bronx, and I went to work as a porter at 1088 Park Avenue, in Manhattan; during this time, I enrolled at Lehman College at the City University of New York. During my college years, I worked full-time and attended school full-time as well. They were long, hard years, but it was well worth it. I was living my dream and embracing everything America had to offer. I even took summer classes to fast-track my graduation; graduating in 1996 with a degree in political science and prelaw. When I was a senior in college, I was promoted to doorman at 525 East Fifty-Seventh Street, the only job I was ever fired from—for being disrespectful to a four-legged furry resident of the building. I'm not sure why people talk to doormen and bartenders, but they do, and you learn some very interesting things.

Mrs. Finer must have been in her late eighties or early nineties and was a permanent fixture in the building for many years. I worked the graveyard shift, so I didn't see her often, but I had heard the stories. During this time, I would leave my post at 7:30 a.m., take the train to college, take a few classes, study at the library for a few hours, and walk home to Morris Park before coming back to work at 11:00 p.m. Needless to say, because of my hours, Mrs. Finer's and my path didn't cross often, but on one fateful day, they did, and it got me into trouble; the best trouble to happen to me because it gave me the boost I needed to leave that job. One morning at about six thirty, Mrs. Finer came to the front desk and began chatting with me about someone who I thought was a relative, Samantha. She explained to me that Samantha was getting older and that she would turn nineteen over the weekend; being an older woman, I brushed off the comment as senility. She described Samantha as brilliant, smart, cute, and told me that she was spending her birthday weekend in Paris and would be returning to New York City in a few days with her trainer; I assumed she was an athlete. I was wrong.

A few days later, I was excited to meet Samantha, who had returned the night before. Working full-time and going to school full-time, I didn't have much of a social life, and I was eager to meet what I assumed was a good-looking girl from high New York society. I made sure I was shaved, put on my best clothes, and brought a book about Western philosophy with me to impress her. I had it all planned, and I was going to try to pursue her, even if it was a long shot. As anticipated, Mrs. Finer came down at 6:30 a.m. with Samantha to introduce me, and much to my surprise, it was not the beautiful nineteen-year-old woman I was expecting, but rather, an ugly old white dog on a leash who I was supposed to walk and pick up after. Mrs. Finer finished our introductions, and out the door I went with Samantha, not the ideal date I had envisioned. My first walk with Samantha ended in disappointment when she broke free and found her way to Harlem. She was lost for a few hours; my job was lost forever. But this was a sign to pursue other opportunities.

After losing my job as a doorman, I finished college and applied for a job in the Giuliani administration and was hired as a fraud investigator focused on white-collar crime and benefit abuse. My job with the City of New York was the best thing to happen to me career-wise; it provided me the opportunity to have a better and more stable income to support my family, provided me enough money to visit Albania a few years later (where I would meet my wife, Mary), and helped me save enough money for law school and discover Fairfield, Connecticut, where I would eventually move and raise my family.

Part 12

MEETING MARY

I n July of 1997, I returned to Albania for the first time since my
escape. The country was in turmoil since the fall of communism,
and our journey promised to be riddled with danger. The country was in the middle of a civil war sparked by former communists
who had just successfully overthrown the Berisha and Democratic
Party government, and no end to the conflict was in sight. At this
point, some of my family had joined us in the United States, but my
brothers Prel and Mark were still living there. Tony and I decided
to take the risk and visit with our brothers. We took a plane from
New York City to Austria and then flew from Austria to Montenegro;
from there, we would find a cab ride to take us across the Albanian
border and take us to the city of Koplik where my brother lived.

The taxi driver, a man in his fifties, looked tired, dejected, and
nervous; he was carrying an AK-47 on his lap. After a few minutes,
both my brother and I realized that he was frantically looking down
at his weapon and looking back at us; he was intently paying attention to our conversation, and we were worried. We had a long ride
ahead of us and had to pass through many more Northern Albanian
villages before arriving in Koplik; the driver was not speaking to us,
even after many attempts to clear the air. We switched our conversation to English and began to make a plan in case things went sour.
Before coming, we had heard from friends that many visitors were
being robbed along various routes to Koplik, Shkoder, and Tirana;

taxi drivers were working with local criminal outfits and coordinating attacks. We decided that if the driver were to leave the main road, we would grab him from behind and choke him to death against the driver's seat with my belt, preventing him from grabbing the gun. After killing the driver, we would take control of the car and his weapon, dump his body, and drive ourselves to Koplik. I removed my belt slowly and held it at its tips, ready to pounce if need be.

When the driver heard us speak English, he inquired in Albanian as to who we were. We complied and told him that we came from the Lumaj family. The car came to a screeching stop; he jumped out of the taxi without his gun and opened my passenger door. Startled, I got out of the car, and he threw his arms around me, crying. He asked my brother to get out. Our taxi driver was my sister's godfather, and with the passage of time, neither he or we recognized each other. A few minutes later, we got back in the car and continued on our journey. We felt safe now. He removed the gun from his lap and passed it to me and asked me if I knew how to use it. I didn't at the time, so I passed it to my brother who had military training.

We arrived in Koplik without any incident, and we immediately went to Prel's house. Our driver walked us upstairs, and we caught Prel's family by surprise. We hadn't told them about our intentions to visit. Nobody recognized each other, but after a few minutes, everything seemed to click. We embraced each other and cried in each other's arms. We reminisced and caught up on each other's lives. The visit was great, and we talked all night.

The following day, at about 5:30 a.m., we woke to the permeating sound of gunfire. The altercation was directly in front of my brother's building, but to this day, we do not know what sparked it. The gunfight ended as quickly as it started, about fifteen minutes long. We could hear the screams and yells of the people in the street. We never ventured outside, but we held up inside by the doors holding AK-47s of our own just in case. In 1997, it seemed everybody in Albania owned an AK-47. Later that morning after the dust of the gunfight had settled, my brother and I left Koplik for Dedaj where we would visit our old family home and my father's grave. The scene of our journey to Dedaj was one of absolute desolation and destruction—the earth looked scorched. As I looked out the window, with my AK-47 in my lap, I could see boys as young as ten or twelve carrying the same weapon I was; what had my country come to? I thought to myself that at any moment, these children could choose to end our lives. It was a terrifying thought. Everybody was playing the same game of mutually assured destruction. It was a quick visit to Dedaj. The drive in convinced us we didn't have time to linger. As we visited our father's grave, we were full of all sorts of emotions, tears, nostalgia, and memories. With no time to waste, we returned to Koplik.

The following day, we went to a coffee shop in downtown Koplik for an afternoon coffee and cocktail. As we walked in, we met one of my old friends from home, Ilir Dashi, who had become the chief of police in town; he was sitting there with two other officers sipping Turkish coffee. We greeted each other and chatted for about five minutes, then I left with my brother to find a different table. A few minutes later, after we had sat down, three men walked into the café with AK-47s and began shooting at Ilir and his colleagues, who returned fire. Bullets were flying, and people were dropping to the floor; my brothers and I took cover behind the counter and waited for the bloodshed to end. As all went quiet, we realized that the commotion had ended; I peeked my head over the counter and saw four bodies scattered across the floor. Two of the assailants were already dead, the other wounded, and Ilir had been shot. Two days later, I attended the funeral of Ilir, who died shortly after the incident.

The continuing commotion in Koplik convinced me and my brother that we needed to think about moving to a new location for the remainder of our stay. We decided to move onto Shkoder to stay with my uncle. There, I would meet my wife, Mary.

One day, while visiting my uncle in Shkoder, I went to the city square with my cousin Mariana for a coffee; while we were chatting and watching the action in the piazza, she mentioned to me that there was a young girl whom she'd admired greatly who was single. As we continued talking, the conversation kept returning to this girl. My cousin obviously had made plans to set me up, and I was interested. The more we talked, the more interested I became. I had no intentions about courtship during my stay, but my mind was made up at this point. I wanted to meet Mary.

The following day, my cousin pressed harder and got the remainder of my family involved. My aunt and uncle were very fond of Mary's parents, and they took it upon themselves to arrange a meeting. As we sat outside discussing the details of our introduction, Mary came by to speak to my cousin and aunt. She was riding a bike and was stunningly beautiful. We said our introductions and talked for a while, and I asked her out on my own terms before my family could get involved. We agreed to meet the following day in the town square for a pizza.

As I approached the table the following day, I could see Mary already sitting. She was all done up, with long, blond hair, crystal-blue eyes, tall, and lovely. I thought to myself, Why am I wasting my time? She is too pretty for me, and this will never work out because in a few weeks, I would have to leave. Regardless of all the thoughts racing through my mind, I sat down anyway; maybe it was excitement, maybe it was curiosity, maybe it was fate. As we sat, ate, and talked, I completely forgot about the war and chaos raging around me; we spent the entire day and most of the evening at the square getting to know each other until it became too late to safely stay out any longer. As she got up to leave, I had the courage to ask her out on another date for the following day, and she said yes. She got on her bike to go home, and I was elated. I had a chance even though she was much better looking than me.

I continued to see Mary every day for a while and eventually asked her to introduce me to her parents because I planned to pop the question. My family and I went over one evening for introductions. After all went well, I asked her father's permission, and he gave me his blessing. A few days later, Mary and I were engaged. I always loved taking risks, but this was the biggest risk I had made to date. Taking risks has always paid off well for me, but this was the biggest reward.

Leaving Mary was the hardest decision I have ever had to make, but I needed to return to the United States. My life was in New York. We kept our engagement, and a year later, she joined me in the United States on an I-130 petition that I filed for her. She has completed me and is the best partner anyone can ask for; she is an amazing wife, mother, and best friend.

Part 13

BECOMING AN ATTORNEY

S hortly after meeting Mary, I decided it was time for me to pursue my next dream and the reason that I wanted to come to the United States in the first place. It was time to go to law school and become an attorney. I was accepted into the law program at Benjamin N. Cardozo School of Law at Yeshiva University, and I began my studies. This was a busy time for us as a family. Mary had come to the United States, and we were newlyweds. I was working full-time in addition to my studies, and we had begun to start a family together. During my time studying, I decided that I wanted to use my education and newly acquired skills to help people who had faced some of the same harsh realities that I had. I wanted to be an immigration attorney who focused on helping people being persecuted by their government regimes for political and religious reasons. My focus would allow me the ability to help people directly within my own community and countless others who experienced many of the same things I did. I graduated in 2007 with a master of laws degree (LLM) and quickly went to work studying for the District of Columbia Bar Exam, which I would need to be able to practice law in federal court. For a short time, I even moved my family to Washington, DC, so I could study there. Many months of studying paid off, and I passed the bar on my second try; I was sworn into the District of Columbia Court of Appeals on December 8, 2008. I have been blessed; today, I run a small successful practice, Law Offices of Lumaj, on Arthur

Avenue in the Bronx and specialize in political and religious asylum cases. I do additional work as well related to immigration, but I am especially enjoying a new firm project—helping women in oversees countries leave abusive marriages. The time commitment of running your own business is exhausting; I often work six days a week and eight to ten hours a day, but I greatly enjoy my work, and I have been fulfilled by it. I found my American dream.

Part 14

ENTRY INTO POLITICS

I have always had a deep-seated interest in politics, both foreign and domestic, but the height of my interest sparked with the ascendency of Barack Obama and the rise of democratic socialism within the Democratic Party of the United States. Over the course of Barack Obama's first term, I watched him and his party work to implement many of the same failed policies that I had left behind in Eastern Europe, and I quickly became concerned for the future of my children and concerned about the direction of my new adopted nation. I could not sit back and idly watch as the identity of the greatest nation on earth slowly eroded into failed socialism. So I got involved. At this point, my family and I had moved to Fairfield, Connecticut, and there was an open United States senate race approaching. After many discussions with my family and friends, testing my potential viability and fund-raising prowess, I decided to put my name forward as an alternative to the candidates that were already in the field on the Republican side. I formally announced my candidacy for the United States Senate on November 23, 2011, and joined the race. I did not anticipate winning the Republican nomination. I was running against former congressman Christopher Shayes, self-funding business magnate, and former 2010 nominee Linda McMahon and a variety of other minor candidates, but I wanted to be part of the discussion. I wanted to put my conservative ideas at the forefront of the debate. At the time, I thought the race lacked a real conservative outsider, and to me, it was important that a conservative viewpoint, which could forcefully warn about the perils of socialism, was heard. I raised a significant amount of money for a first-time candidate, but unfortunately, my candidacy never really caught fire. The Republican Party apparatus was ready to crown Linda McMahon for a second time, whom I went on to endorse and campaign for in the general election. McMahon went on to lose that election after spending an excess of $100 million between her two unsuccessful runs for US Senate. But she ran a strong campaign and remained involved, helping Republicans throughout Connecticut and the nation in subsequent election cycles; I grew to have tremendous respect for Lina and her family. Later, McMahon would accept a position with the Trump administration, running the Small Business Association, and would go on to do an amazing job helping grow small businesses throughout the United States.

Like McMahon, after my defeat at the Connecticut Republican Party Convention in 2012, I decided to remain involved in the party while considering my future as a potential candidate for office in Connecticut. I began a statewide tour and immersed myself in local Connecticut politics, helping anyone and everyone who asked for it; I began raising money for the state and local Republican Parties, made telephone calls, knocked doors, and participated in numerous speaking engagements. Our success of the party at the local level in 2012 convinced me that there was a path for a potential statewide candidacy for me in 2014, and I once again began deliberations with my family and friends. After months of consultation and talks with local Republican and conservative activists, I announced my candidacy for the Republican nomination for secretary of state on February 13, 2013. This campaign would mark my success or failure within Republican Party politics in Connecticut, so I needed to run this race well and put up a strong showing. The beginning of the campaign was a family affair focused on raising small-dollar donations to qualify for the state's generous campaign financing program; I toured the state and focused almost all my time meeting potential contributors and maintaining relationships that I had made in 2012. In October of 2013, I hired Brock Weber, a local political operative who had a résumé that consisted of political work ranging from local Board of Education races to presidential races, to be my campaign manager, and we ramped the campaign into high gear. Brock is part of my political operation to this day, and we have become dear friends.

In Connecticut, under-ticket races don't get much attention, but 2014 was different. After the gains made by the Republicans in the legislature the last two election cycles, Republicans could smell blood in the water, and high-quality candidates for all offices were coming out of the woodwork. Our immediate task as a campaign was to present me as a viable candidate and raise an insurmountable amount of money to keep others from jumping into the secretary of state's race. I was never the darling of the state Republican leadership. I was viewed as too conservative by most, and many within the party had issues with me challenging their preferred candidates and not waiting my turn to run for office; they were intent on forcing me out of the race at all costs and actively worked against both me and my campaign. As a result, Brock and I made the decision to take our message directly to the people and began an intense schedule of meeting with local Republican town committees and potential delegates ahead of the 2014 Republican Party State Convention. As we crisscrossed the state, we could see momentum growing; delegates began pledging to me at a record rate, endorsements began flowing, and the uptick in our fund-raising continued to grow daily. My success worried many within the party, and their resolve to force me out strengthened. At this point several people within party leadership had asked me to consider withdrawing my candidacy. They had threatened my political future, and they were actively trying to recruit a candidate to oppose me. Their efforts in the long run would fail, but by early spring of 2014, they had finally found a challenger to oppose me for the Republican Party nomination—Michael McDonald, a former town councilman from Windsor, Connecticut. During the course of the campaign, I came to know and like Mike very much, but he never really presented a large threat to our campaign; he joined the race very late and had serious issues with fund-raising. Our strategy and hard work had paid off. My campaign more or less had the party endorsement wrapped up in February of 2014, three months ahead of the scheduled convention. Our success was gratifying, but now we had another mission—collect enough delegates to deny McDonald and give the party leadership an opportunity to prime me for the nomination in August; under Connecticut state law, any candidate who receives 15 percent of the delegate votes at a party convention or collects an appropriate number of qualifying signatures can challenge the party-endorsed candidate in a primary election. Our campaign continued at a hard and fast pace all the way up to the convention. At the end, I had visited 110 Republican town committees and was within a few thousand dollars of qualifying for the state grant, far ahead of my opposition and far ahead of many running for the various other state offices. Finally, the day of the vote came at the convention being held at Mohegan Sun Casino, and we were victorious. I won the Connecticut Republican Party endorsement and nomination with over 86 percent of the vote and was able to deny McDonald a spot on the primary ballot. I was elated. Many within the leadership were visibly angry, but the delegates had spoken, and I was their choice.

After taking a short two-day break, my team reassembled at our headquarters and we set off to begin our general election campaign. The general election had a much different tone than the nomination battle. The party rallied around my candidacy, helped me raise the reminder of the donations needed to qualify for the general election grant, and was very helpful in everything we asked for. This was supposed to be our year, and the party was in high spirits; all the Republican candidates had even qualified for the Independent Party endorsement, meaning our ticket would now appear on two lines of the ballot, competing directly with the Democrats and the cross-endorsing, socialist-leaning Working Families Party. We ran an aggressive campaign, invested in all the typical things you would expect— direct mail, television and radio advertising—but we were also doing something very different, something that would set us apart. In addition to the nuts and bolts of the typical under-ticket campaign, Brock and I had made an early determination to invest heavily in field operations and direct voter contact. We had an impressive ground game and were coordinating closely with Connecticut Republican

Party operations. My field team led by Deputy Campaign Manager Jennifer Krantz, Field Director James McGill, and Office Manager Cassandra Dudzinski were making thousands of voter contacts daily through phone operations and door-to-door canvassing; my voter registration team overseen by Besa Kalici was identifying thousands of potential new Republican voters in communities not typically targeted by the party, and we were making substantial progress. This race was going to be closer than anyone expected. Polling showed us making considerable gains. We were running a close race with incumbent Denise Merrill. We knew it; the party knew it. Now, if we could only convince the media. We did everything within our power to convince the media that the race was much closer than they had anticipated, but they weren't budging. They were now our biggest obstacle.

Despite the chosen ignorance of the media, we kept moving forward, running our race on our own terms. I put tens of thousands of miles on my car, personally knocked thousands of doors, attended hundreds of events, and shook what felt like a million hands. Campaigning is an exhausting but truly gratifying experience; exhausting because of the sheer work and hours it consumes, but gratifying because of the people you meet and the stories you hear. I love the campaign trail more than most and seriously miss its romance and intensity. About halfway through October, the tide greatly turned in our favor. We received the coveted endorsement of the Norwich Bulletin, and the media realized that they had overlooked an important, now competitive, statewide race. The final two weeks of the campaign were a blur to me. Our schedule and news coverage tripled, other newspapers began endorsing our campaign, and the buzz about Republican upsets up and down the ticket consumed every ounce of political discourse throughout the state. As we steamrolled across Connecticut the final weekend of the campaign on our scheduled Republican ticket bus tour, the magnitude of the possibility of winning set in. I, this little-known political newcomer from Northern Albania, was on the cusp of potentially being elected Connecticut secretary of state, potentially upsetting one of the most powerful, well-known women in Connecticut politics. The thought consumed me, and I was awestruck.

I arrived at the headquarters on election night full of hope and optimism but thoroughly tired. We were watching the returns come in with the Connecticut Republican Party in Greenwich but had a private war room located on the third floor. The night started out very promising, and we built an early and sizable lead. But two problems were making themselves evidently clear. Cities were not reporting any numbers at all yet, and it looked like independent turnout was depressed in every corner of the state. Connecticut, being a reliably blue state, is very hard for a Republican to win, but depressed independent turnout makes it almost impossible. The negativity of the gubernatorial election had turned the contest into a base election, and that hurt statewide Republican prospects all throughout the state. We held the lead in the vote count until about 3:00 a.m. the following day, then New Haven reported. Republicans typically get crushed in New Haven, but Democratic efforts in the city led by Governor Malloy's reelection team and President Obama's Organizing for America had spiked turnout to levels never before seen in Connecticut. The election was over not just for me but for the whole ticket. Republicans lost every statewide race in 2014. It was our race to lose, and we lost it. Though I was disappointed I lost, I was proud of our work and the many accomplishments of my campaign. We performed better than most of the candidates I ran with statewide, and our countless efforts in Connecticut's inner cities yielded impressive results for a Republican. We had ran one of the most competitive under-ticket races in modern Connecticut political history and shocked the local Connecticut political world, and I was satisfied. Shortly after my loss in 2014, I began fielding calls about potential political prospects in 2016 and 2018; I had impressed enough people with my secretary of state showing to make me an immediate contender for a potential future political run, and that brought a smile to my face.

Campaigns can take a lot of people, and I was in no rush to make a determination on what my future held. I was incredibly grateful to be given the opportunity to be a nominee of the Republican Party, and I felt I owed a great deal to the people who supported me. So just as before, I returned to the trenches and spent the next couple of years working on behalf of the party and countless Republican candidates all across Connecticut. I maintained an active schedule in addition to my work in the private sector, so much so that it actually felt like a second job, but I was glad to do it. Work began again—fund-raising, making phone calls, knocking doors, and delivering speeches. At this point, my profile had raised significantly with Republican Party circles, and demand was high. I started a local weekly radio program on 1490 WGCH AM out of Greenwich, Connecticut, to spread my conservative philosophy, and I was having the time of my life. Politics was now a regular entity in the Lumaj household and consumed nearly all my free and non-free time. As 2016 came and went, I was enthralled by Donald Trump's candidacy for president and became a vocal supporter of his campaign, his agenda, and his eventual presidency. He brought a brash and unapologetic approach to politics and governance, and despite some of his personal flaws, it was refreshing. Connecticut needed the approach Trump brought to the United States, and he was a major reason I decided to give running again some consideration.

I had taken some steps in early 2016 to leave the door open to a possible run in 2018, but I was far from a decision. I left my weekly program at the radio station to devote more time to helping the local Republican town committees and candidates, and I began regular talks and discussions with my core group of supporters and my campaign staff from 2014. We were eying a statewide run again but hadn't made a final determination if we would be looking at a federal or state race. After many months of consultation, encouragement, and deliberation, we made the determination to explore potential candidacies for secretary of state and for governor, with a heavy emphasis on determining viability for a potential gubernatorial race in 2018. On September 6, 2016, accompanied by supporters and staff, I was the first person to file an exploratory committee with the Connecticut State Enforcement Commission to explore a possible statewide race in 2018. Connecticut exploratory committees allow potential candidates the ability to asses viability, raise and expend monies, and begin the onerous process of qualifying for the state's Citizens Election Program, a public financing of political campaigns. As soon as the paperwork was filed, we would embark upon a seventeen-month journey to the Connecticut Republican Party State Convention. It was a daunting task, but I was up for the challenge.

Like 2014, viability was our primary concern. A gubernatorial race was much different from an under-ticket race; the quality of opposing candidates would be different, and the money needed to be competitive would be much higher. For us to be viable, we needed to start early and have multiple early successes. My name ID among the delegate class was strong because of my previous runs for office and from years of tending to various relationships statewide, but we needed to get started on the money right away; soon, other candidates with similar strengths would be competing for the same dollars we were. I started collecting the low-hanging fruit, and we began the process of organizing our first major fundraiser, which would be held in the Bronx with family, friends, and associates. It was a huge success. When we reported our fund-raising numbers at the end of 2016, we were the fund-raising leader, outraising Mark Boughton, the Mayor of Danbury, twice a candidate for governor before and the presumptive favorite for the 2018 nomination 4–1.

We roared into 2017 with momentum on our side, and for the first time since filing our paperwork, we were being treated as a major contender for the Republican nomination for governor. The next few months were exactly what you would expect—time fund-raising and time visiting the circuit of local party activists and potential delegates. We were working hard to amass support and were deep in the process of putting together a strong campaign steering committee and honing in on an eventual campaign message. Over the course of spring, the remainder of the Republican field started to take shape, and we were anxiously waiting on a decision from Democratic Governor Dan Malloy on whether or not he would seek reelection to a third term. Malloy, plagued by low approval ratings, opted against reelection in mid-April, and that decision blew the race wide open; what was thought to be a typical race at first became very crowded and confusing on both sides within a matter of weeks. Everybody was running or at least actively considering it. Regardless of the outside forces shaping the overall tone of the race, our exploratory effort was going well. We were raising exploratory and qualifying money at a consistent pace. We were polling well among potential delegates, and we were performing well in various straw polls being held by the local Republican town committees, often coming within the top three and winning our fair share. We were exactly where we needed to be at this point. It was starting to become evident that an eventual campaign for governor was likely to happen.

We went into the summer of 2017 as one of the top three favorites for the party endorsement at the convention, but an ever-growing and crowded Republican field was making the prospects of winning the convention outright less likely every day. We refined our strategy to focus on qualifying for a primary election through the convention process and taking our message directly to the voters if we decided to pull the trigger and make our campaign official. The pursuit of fund-raising money dominated our campaign in late summer of 2017; we were doing exceptionally well raising exploratory funds and had more or less reached our goal at this point, but qualifying in-state money had started to slow, and we needed to pick up the pace to remain competitive with our opponents, many of whom had skipped an exploratory stage and were laser focused on hitting only one threshold. We took a risk and threw a Hail Mary; we would invest heavily in a fiftieth birthday party for me within the very large Albanian community in Waterbury, Connecticut. A one-night event full of music, food, and booze; we needed it to pay off. Preparations for the event consumed every ounce of staff time in late August and early September. They worked with leaders of the community, specifically Ray Etemi, to bring in famous Albanian singers in from oversees. They began an aggressive presale of tickets to get an accurate headcount and worked with the Albanian American Center to figure out the logistics of liquor and food for what we were hoping would be five hundred people. As the day of the party approached, we were all nervous. Failure here could result in the end of our campaign; success would mean that we could move forward. We were hoping to raise $50,000 in one night—a never-before-seen feat in history of the Citizens Election Program. The event blew away all expectations; nearly seven hundred people showed up to participate, and my campaign raised almost $70,000 in one evening. The event saved our campaign and gave us the final push we needed to make a final decision on formally entering the gubernatorial race as a declared candidate.

On November 19, 2017, I held a final exploratory steering committee meeting with staff and key supporters throughout Connecticut at our headquarters in Southington. We went through the pros and cons of entering the race formally and discussed our fund-raising status, the challenges of raising the remaining money needed, and the ever-changing dynamics of the race unfolding. The race was crowded, but our efforts benefited from a core group of dedicated conservative supporters in the state, many of whom were likely to be delegates—my political director, Sean Cleary; my field director, Joe Hoxha; and my office manager, Cassandra Dudzinski, facilitated the discussion as my campaign manager, again, Brock Weber, looked on. As we went around the room, everybody gave their two cents. After hearing everybody's thoughts, concerns, encouragement, and excitement, we made the decision. We were going to run, and we would formally file with the State Election Enforcement Commission within the next ten days.

Jumping into an already crowded field meant that we needed to boost political operations as quickly as possible. We had done plenty of legwork throughout the exploratory process, but now it was crunch time, and we needed a full court press on potential delegates while we maintained our regular operations. Over the next few months, our team grew to include Juliana Simone, a 2014 employee who came on to help with communications; Joe Violet and Gregg Hannan, to help with field operations; Joe Kilduff, our treasurer; and a plethora of dedicated and hungry interns who helped make direct voter contacts with influence makers and delegates. We were fighting for 15 percent at the convention, and the outlook observed was good. Moving into a formal candidate committee also finally gave us leeway to start rolling out some high-profile endorsements we had been courting in the exploratory process and the ability to be more vocal about our intentions, platform, and issues.

The next few months were routine. The typical series of motions any campaign would make ahead of a political convention; finalizing fund-raising, direct potential delegate communication, Republican town committee meetings and events. But this year, the state party was also doing something different. The major candidates for governor were invited to a series of five debates, one in each congressional district, to give the delegates and the press an in-depth look at their candidacies, their views, and their arguments of electability. It was an intriguing process and one that I made the most of, often being the aggressor to draw sharp contrast between myself and my opponents. After all, with the field being overcrowded, we needed another way to stand out. The debates opened the convention endorsement process to political handicappers in a way never before seen in Connecticut politics; for the first time, the media was actually talking about front-runners and also-rans based on in-depth analysis and feedback instead of just pulling complete and utter bullshit out of thin air. They were talking about us as a front-runner, which was both good and bad for our campaign. Front-runner status gives you a lot of attention in the media, but it also puts a big target on your back; come spring of 2018, I was being hit by the media and by my opponents almost every day, and it was starting to affect the campaign.

Math was becoming important. There are only so many delegates elected to attend the Republican State Convention, and we were doing everything within our power to make sure we received at least 15 percent on the first ballot to qualify for the primary election. Crowded fields make conventions very difficult endeavors. Our campaign was teetering on the edge of fifteen all spring; it seemed to us that we had a very high floor in comparison to most campaigns, but our ceiling was low. We were fighting for second place with Tim Herbst on the first ballot and assuming Boughton would come out on top but not by much. We were very confident in our projections, but mudslinging by my opponents, some within party leadership and the media, was taking a toll. As I had said before, I had never been the favorite of the Connecticut Republican Party leadership or the media. They seemed intent on thwarting our efforts and were actively engaging in a shadow campaign with some of my opponents to knock me out of contention. We did the best we could to respond to some of the ridiculous accusations, misrepresentations, and mischaracterizations they put in front of the delegates, but honestly, it was hard to keep up with the almost daily falsehoods being spread about me, my background, my positions, and my campaign. Nevertheless, we powered on; focused on our message of conservative values and the need for a Hartford outsider, we were taking our campaign directly to the delegates.

The convention at Foxwoods Casino arrived, and I couldn't have been more nervous and at the same time more excited. Our projections had us over 15 percent, but not by much. Holding our existing support became our major concern. I worked thoroughly with my staff the entire first day to make the rounds as often as I could to meet and greet, shake hands, and convince any last-minute, undecided delegates. We held receptions, get-togethers, and cocktail hours with my supporters and the undecideds to sway them to stay or join us; we did everything within our power to win, but unfortunately the next day, we would come up just short.

I met with my staff early the next morning for a final strategy brief and updated delegate count. The numbers hadn't moved much since the night before, but it looked like we had picked up some new votes largely due to the hard work Gregg Hannan had put into the third congressional district—some good news. After the meeting, I went downstairs to our breakfast reception and began pressing the flesh for the last time before the vote. Walking the corridor outside the convention hall was a sight to see. Roughly 1,200 Republican Party activist culminated on the final day of voting, ready to determine their standard bearer. Anxiety came over my entire body; this was the day. Months on the road campaigning, tens of thousands of miles on my car, nearly half a million dollars raised (still the CEP record) would all come down to this. I was being accompanied by Brock when he got a phone call. We had a problem with Southington. Southington was a large delegation that we identified for us and was a major piece of the math that got us to 15 percent; we had to act quickly. This wasn't the first time Southington had done this to us this campaign or even this weekend. I was getting tired of going to them and pleading, and I was getting nervous.

An hour later, my campaign had resolved the immediate Southington problem, but an odd lingering feeling of betrayal remained with me. We entered the convention hall shortly after the vote started to take place. There was little time to watch results come in as a candidate. You needed to be vigilant in your floor operations with you staff, talking to key people, visiting with target delegations, and hand-holding anyone whom you feel may be wavering. Ballots can take anywhere from one hour to an hour and a half, and it is an exhausting process. You need to be conscious of your count, know where you've lost identified delegates, and hone in on areas you think you can peel some people off other candidates for yourself. During the first ballot, our numbers were holding steady, but we had lost some votes and were coming in under our original projections. It's amazing to think that people who have guaranteed you their vote are willing to do so while blatantly lying to your face, but I suppose that's just politics. Small numbers added up, and by the time we had reached the last congressional district on the first ballot, I could see that 15 percent was not going to happen on the first ballot. We had fallen shy by just three votes.

On the first ballot, we had come in third place out of the original eight major names placed into nomination, following closely behind Tim Herbst in second and Mark Boughton in first. They were the only two candidates who had received enough support to the primary of the first ballot, but both were far from a majority. Chaos and confusion riddled the convention floor as we headed into the second ballot. Some candidates had been eliminated, but the generous convention rules kept the second ballot almost the same. As the roll was called for the second time, the balloting began. I'm not going to bore you with the minutia of the second ballot. The results didn't differ much with the exception of the top two gaining ground and Steve Obsitnik, surprising everyone, coming in third. My campaign's results remained steady. We picked up a few votes and lost a few votes and even looked like we would potentially get over the threshold, but just as I predicted, Southington left at the very last minute, and we were knocked out of contention, coming within just a few votes for a second time.

Disappointment is not enough to describe the feeling of coming so close, but yet being so far away. I had poured my heart and soul into my campaign for governor, and I was upset. My team was upset, my supporters were upset. Politics is a dirty sport, and it's not for the faint of heart. I wish the result would've been different, but maybe in the end, I was the lucky one. Months later, as primary season approached, a little-known, self-funding businessman, Bob Stefanowski, who had skipped the convention process by way of nominating petition, blew the competition away in the primary and came out as the eventual Republican nominee for governor. I actively supported Stefanowski in the primary, endorsed him after my campaign folded, campaigned with him, recorded robocalls on his behalf, and appeared on campaign mailers for him. He was a conservative outsider like me, and that was what Hartford needed. Unfortunately Stefanowski would go on to lose a close general election to Democrat Ned Lamont, and Connecticut would continue its steady decline into the void.

I don't know if I'll ever run for office again. The toll it takes on you, your supporters, your friends, and your family is daunting. However, the chances I had to run for office in the greatest country on earth were the highlights of my life outside the confines of my family. I am eternally grateful for the opportunities the United States of America has presented to me over the course of my time here. In my opinion, one doesn't truly understand the greatness of our nation until you have lived a life like mine. I am happy and proud of the life I am living. I am proud of my background and history. I am proud of my struggles and of my accomplishments, and I am eager to see what the future holds for me and my family. For the time being, I am content living the American dream.

2a - An avid Second Amendment Supporter, Lumaj
attends the CCDL Legislative Workshop and Shooting
event in Simsbury, CT. He is pictured with supporter
Tippawan Cleary in the photo montage.

2014 campaign - A Lumaj for Secretary of the
State sign on a beautiful fall day in Avon, CT.

2016 cycle - Lumaj and team help 2016 Republican candidates on Election Day 2016.

2017 cycle - Lumaj and team help 2017 Republican candidates on Election Day 2017.

accepting nomination— Peter Lumaj accepts the
Republican nomination for Secretary of the State at the
2014 CTGOP State Convention at Mohegan Sun.

Albanian fest— Peter Lumaj talks with a voter at the
2014 Albanian Festival in Waterbury, CT. Lumaj
is joined by CTGOP Gubernatorial nominee, Tom
Foley and State Senate nominee Karl Shehu.

"I came here as a refugee. The first job I held was flipping burgers. I started with nothing — not a penny when I came to the United States, but I went to night school and eventually became a lawyer. Anyone can realize his dream if he is willing to work."

— PETER LUMAJ, CANDIDATE FOR GOVERNOR

Barkhamsted GOP backs Lumaj for governor

BY KATHRYN BOUGHTON
REPUBLICAN-AMERICAN

BARKHAMSTED — The Republican Town Committee has thrown its support behind gubernatorial candidate Peter Lumaj.

Lumaj, who ran for secretary of state in 2014 and U.S. Senate in 2012, appeared before the committee on Monday night to explain his campaign positions.

Barkhamsted Town Committee Chairwoman Jahana Simone, who is Lumaj's director of communications, said the local committee has strongly supported the candidate for years.

"I have always admired his deep love for this country and the individual freedoms it offers to its citizens," she wrote on the committee's website.

In his presentation, Lumaj encouraged Republicans to be proud and to own their allegiance to President Donald Trump.

"We have no reason to be ashamed of being Republicans," he said. "I think it's the reason we lost in 2014 — gubernatorial candidate Tom Foley was ashamed to be a rich, white guy. Isn't that the entire reason to live in a free country — to do better? We had the same problem with Mitt Romney. If we do it again, the Democrats will smell weakness."

He said Republicans have "done a poor job in defining ourselves. We have been defined by the media. We cower in the corner and defend ourselves. We've not had it at all. If we were a racist party, I wouldn't be here tonight."

He contends that President Trump won because, despite his wealth, he connected with the common people.

"The Trump base in our state, a large percentage didn't vote Republican before. He identified with them," Lumaj said. "His character is to fight for what he believes in. I stick by those principals of Trump voters. There is no reason to run away from that."

RTC MEMBER DAVID MOULTON asked how Lumaj, an attorney from the Bronx, N.Y., with a home in Fairfield, would connect with voters.

"I work with a lot of blue-collar men and hardly are [...] voted for Foley or Romney," Moulton said. "They said, 'He's the rich guy, he doesn't care about me.' How do you convince these guys on the shop floor to vote for you?"

Lumaj referred to his own history, which includes escaping from Communist Albania nearly 30 years ago and making his way to the U.S. He worked as a porter and doorman to help support his family, and to pay for his education at the City University of New York, where he earned a degree in political science.

"I came here as a refugee," he said. "The first job I held was flipping burgers. I started with nothing — not a penny when I came to the United States, but I went to night school and eventually became a lawyer. Anyone can realize his dream if he is willing to work."

Lumaj said he can identify with the middle class.

"Most Republicans can identify with the middle class if properly approached," he added. "Wealth doesn't define you."

Lumaj's platform is decidedly aligned with Trump. He pronounces himself a "Second Amendment guy," opposes amnesty for illegal aliens and condemns "sanctuary cities" that are sheltering them. He criticizes Connecticut's welfare system, saying illegal aliens should be ineligible for benefits.

"IT PAYS TO BE ILLEGAL, and come to our state," he said. "People are moving into this state that are barely producing anything. If you join welfare today, you will make more than $40,000 a year without doing anything. The Democrats want government dependency. Look at the crime rate, the unemployment rate. [...] Republicans should point out that everything (Democrats) touched is broken. We are the party of solutions."

Lumaj said he believes tax relief is the key to kick-starting the state's recovery.

"I think we have to start with tax relief so people have more money," he said, adding "you could feel the economy change right away" after Congress passed its tax reform.

"How do you defend against the charge that it is making the deficit worse?" Moulton asked.

"First thing you have to accept is that the Democrats will blame us," Lumaj replied. "But we have to say, 'We tried your methods and it got worse. Let's try ours.' As Republicans, we have to say we will uphold our agreements with the voters. We should be very forceful about these things."

Lumaj said his greatest weakness — a lack of gubernatorial experience — also can be seen as a strength.

"Professional politicians are thinking of getting elected and using that as a steppingstone," he said. "I am not looking for a promotion. I could practice law and be happy with it."

He said he has enjoyed a positive reception as he tours the state. Lumaj noted that three of the 10 Republican candidates — Danbury Mayor Mark Boughton, former Trumbull First Selectman Timothy Herbst and himself — are polling in double digits.

"This election is ours to lose," he said.

KATHRYN BOUGHTON/REPUBLICAN-AMERICAN

Gubernatorial candidate Peter Lumaj addresses the Barkhamsted Republican Town Committee on Monday night.

barkhamsted GOP endorse— A local newsclip from The Waterbury Republican-American discussing the Barkhamsted Republican Town Committee's endorsement of Lumaj's candidacy for governor in 2018.

Benghazi— Peter Lumaj with Benghazi hero and survivor Kris "Tanto" Paronto at a CTGOP event Lumaj helped sponsor.

brothers— Peter and the Lumaj brothers
relax with family and friends.

campaign fair— Lumaj meeting voters at a local fair in 2014.

campaign trail—Lumaj participating in a variety of
campaign trail events in the summer of 2017.

ccdl rally—Lumaj waiting for his turn to speak
in front of the CCDL rally in 2014.

cleary fundraiser— Photo montage of the "First Annual
Holiday Party" event held at the home of Dennis and Eileen
Cleary to benefit the 2018 Lumaj Exploratory Committee.

commercial shoot—Photo still of 2014 campaign commercial shoot at Noujaim Tool Company in Waterbury, CT.

debate 1—Photo montage of pictures taken at the Second CTGOP Gubernatorial Debate held in Hebron, CT

doors waterbury—Lumaj breaks for a bit of fun while
campaigning door-to-door with staff in Waterbury, CT.

early returns 2014— Lumaj celebrates "strong" early
returns with staff on election night in 2014.

eday 14— Lumaj meets with supporters in Bridgeport, CT at a polling location on Election Day 2014.

eday 14_2 - Lumaj meets with supporters in Waterbury, CT at a polling location on Election Day 2014.

eric trump— Lumaj greets Eric Trump, son of President Donald Trump, at a local Republican fundraising event in Greenwich, CT.

Face the state— Lumaj appearing on Face the State with Dennis House during the 2018 gubernatorial campaign.

Fair Brooklyn—Lumaj meeting with voters and
campaign staff at the 2014 Brooklyn, CT Fair.

fairfield—Lumaj making get-out-the-vote calls for
Fairfield, CT Republican candidates in 2015.

family beach—Lumaj posing for a photo with
his children on a family vacation.

farmington 14—Lumaj poses with supporters at a get-out-
the-vote rally the night before the election in 2014.

father—Peter's father, Prek Lumaj.

filing paperwork—Lumaj files his official exploratory
paperwork for the 2018 election in September of 2016.
Lumaj is joined by supporters State Senator Joe Markley, State
Rep. Rob Sampson, CTGOP State Central Committeman
Dennis Cleary and Office Manager Cassandra Dudzinski.

frank's grad—Lumaj joined by his family at
his son's high school graduation.

gop team 14—Lumaj joins candidates, supporters and
activists for a post-parade picture in Newtown, CT in 2014.

greenwich—Lumaj looks on, waiting to speak, at a local Republican fundraising event in Greenwich, CT.

harding—Lumaj poses with Steven Harding and Dan Carter at a special election event held in Bethel, CT.

independent party—Lumaj poses for a photo after receiving the
Independent Party of Connecticut endorsement in 2014. Lumaj
ran on both the Republican and Independent lines in the 2014
and was also endorsed by the Justice Party of Connecticut.

Italian fest—Lumaj poses for a picture at the Our Lady
of Mount Carmel Church Italian Festival in 2014.

ledyard steak out—Lumaj amps up the Republican troops at the annual Ledyard Steak Out in 2015.

lincoln day dinner—Lumaj poses for a picture at the 2015 Plymouth Lincoln Day Dinner after delivering the keynote address. Lumaj is pictured with Chairman Bob Ives, Mayor David Merchant, State Senator Henri Martin and State Rep. Whit Betts.

lori—Lumaj is interviewed by Lori Hopkins-Cavanagh on 94.9 WJJF broadcasting to eastern Connecticut.

mayor for the day—Lumaj holds up a cake celebrating his appointment as Albanian Mayor for the day in Waterbury, CT.

mum parade—Lumaj supporters Victoria Passmore,
Lauren Dudzinski and Cassandra Dudzinski take a selfie
before starting the 2014 Mum Parade in Bristol, CT.

parade—Lumaj staff and volunteers join Peter
as he marches in a parade in 2014.

Parade moosup—Frank Lumaj holds his totem high
in the 2014 VJ Day Parade in Moosup, CT.

phones 14—Lumaj joins volunteers making voter
ID calls ahead of the 2014 general election.

plymouth fundraiser—Photo montage of the Plymouth Republican Town Committee's Fundraiser to support the 2018 Lumaj exploratory committee. Plymouth was the first RTC to endorse Lumaj in both the 2014 and 2018 election cycles.

rally—Photo montage of the rally to support Lumaj before the third CTGOP Gubernatorial Debate held in West Haven, CT.

real story—Lumaj appearing on The Real Story
discussing his campaign for governor.

rnc convention—Lumaj attending the first day's events
of the 2016 Republican National Convention.

show prep—Lumaj preparing for his radio program
"On Point with Peter Lumaj" in the spring of 2016.

staff birthday—Lumaj surprised by his former
staffers celebrating his 48th birthday.

Steering— Lumaj poses with members of his 2018 exploratory committee's (Lumaj Explore) steering committee.

trump ball—Photo montage of the Lumaj's attending one of the inaugural balls for President Donald Trump in January of 2017.

uconn—Lumaj's campaign for governor attracted a significant amount of youth support. A local newsclip from The Daily Campus discussing the UCONN College Republican's endorsement of Lumaj's candidacy for governor in 2018.

Wedding –Lumaj with his bride, Mary Lumaj, the day of their wedding.

Westport—Lumaj rallies the Republican troops in Westport, CT ahead of the 2014 general election.

PART II, PETER'S ESSAYS

Essays

PROLOGUE

The following essays were compiled and edited immediately before the GOP Convention of 2016, by far the single most significant election for the American Union since Reagan's election in 1980. I had selected a score of topics ranging from macroeconomics, international finance, political economy, and history to Connecticut's dreadful news of having General Electric quit Connecticut for Boston. These chosen topics serve to elucidate a profound moral dilemma—namely, the bankrupting of our current political order and the dominant political class that underwrites it.

The immediate question at hand cries for a solution, but no solution is at hand if we maintain the status quo of confiscatory taxation, cash transfers, and redistribution while neglecting the very solution that would liberate citizens to pursue their God-given right to equity and capital formation—namely, federalism.

The solution to Connecticut's domestic fiscal, social problems isn't found in government, it is discerned in recognizing enduring first principles. The family is the basic unit of Western civilization, not militant autonomy. Growth matters—as does sound money and statesmanship—in deterring immediate threats while strengthening the union. Connecticut's dominant political class cannot, will not, consecrate itself to this charge, that it defends its constitutive place in the American Union.

The threats that dominate contemporary life are born inside the house of liberty itself. This is a very old conflict, one that predates the founding of the American Union, but it has finally arrived and must be confronted if we are to prosper and not decline. There are sources to fortify our engagement. Tocqueville comes to mind, but so does John Paul II, Alexander Solzhenitsyn, Irving Kristol, John Podhoretz, Reagan, and Thatcher, just to name a few who survived this conflict.

The truth is that America alone remains the last best home for humanity. Our role in maintenance of international order is indispensable, and we ignore that role at our own peril. The world's monetary system is based on the US dollar. The US Navy maintains order for the international commons, free of charge. Ask other nation-states whom they want as a partner in the maintenance of order, be it Saudi Arabia, Russia, or Pakistan. They all point to Washington. We cannot repudiate our role, but we can help constrain threats. We can foster institutions that sustain leadership.

This book examines the state of order and the dominant, failed political class that has wrecked the American Union; only a return to first principles can save us now.

American Exceptionalism Is Freedom and Liberty and Nothing Else

As I integrated myself into the American way of life, I heard a lot about American exceptionalism and began pondering over it. What is American exceptionalism? Does it mean Americans are better than others or that God loves us, Americans, more than others? What does it mean? I began reading and researching about this topic, and eventually I settled with the explanation I read from Rush Limbaugh.

> Anyway, what American exceptionalism is not: It is not that we are better people. It is not that we are superior people. It is not that we are smarter people. It is not that God loves us and hates everybody else.

It is not that God prefers us. It is not that God doesn't prefer anybody else.

American exceptionalism has nothing to do with anything but freedom and liberty. Here is what American exceptionalism is. So what is it? Well, if you know the history of the world. Read your Bible, read whatever historical account of humanity you hold dear, and what you'll read about is human tyranny. You'll read of bondage. You'll read of slavery. The vast majority of the people, the vast majority of the human beings who have lived and breathed and walked this planet have lived under the tyranny of despots, the vast majority.

It isn't even close. The vast majority of the people of this world since the beginning of time have never known the kind of liberty and freedom that's taken for granted every day in this country. Most people have lived in abject fear of their leaders. Most people have lived in abject fear of whoever held power over them. Most people in the world have not had plentiful access to food and clean water. It was a major daily undertaking for most people to come up with just those two basic things.

Just surviving was the primary occupation of most people in the world. The history of the world is dictatorship, tyranny, subjugation, whatever you want to call it, of populations—and then along came the United States of America. Pilgrims were the first to come here seeking freedom from all that. They were oppressed because of their religion. They were told they had to believe in the king and his god, whatever it was, or they would be imprisoned.

They led an exodus from Europe to this country, people of the same mind-set. They simply wanted to escape the tyranny of their ordinary lives. This country was founded that way. For the first time in human history, a government and country was founded on the belief that leaders serve the population. This country was the first in history, the exception—e-x-c-e-p-t, except. The exception to the rule is what American exceptionalism is.

It is because of this liberty and freedom that our country exists, because the founders recognized it comes from God. It's part of the natural yearning of the human spirit. It is not granted by a government. It's not granted by any other human being. We are created with the natural yearning to be free, and it is other men and leaders throughout human history who have suppressed that and imprisoned people for seeking it.

The US is the first time in the history of the world where a government was organized with a Constitution laying out the rules, that the individual was supreme and dominant, and that is what led to the US becoming the greatest country ever because it's unleashed people to be the best they could be. Nothing like it had ever happened. That's American exceptionalism.

Millions of Americans understand exactly and precisely what American exceptionalism is, and that is why they are so appalled about this administration. That is why they are so appalled and opposed to Obamacare, Obama's economic policies, amnesty, illegal immigration with impunity. It's because it is a direct assault on the very foundation and fundamentals of the creation and the founding of this country. That is why there's such opposition to Obama. It has nothing to do with he's black and nothing to do with he's inexperienced. It's because he is conducting an assault on the founding of this country for the purposes of transforming it in ways that would turn us into subjects to government, just like every other person in this planet.

The Politics of State Income Tax or Socialism in Connecticut

Connecticut is very much like the rest of the Northeast. Poor, fiscally profligate, heavily taxed blue states are simply broken, and governors throughout the union are seeking to build political constituencies favorable to capital, equity formation. Let's review.

Nine states have no state income tax. Kansas and Oklahoma have lowered their rates with the aim of elimination altogether. Both Indiana and North Carolina aim to prioritize tax reform in light of a net loss of state citizens moving out of blue states toward localities advertising progrowth agendas. Even once heavily Democratic states like New Mexico are seeking to slash state corporate taxes. Ditto for Nebraska and Louisiana. These governors are looking at the impact taxation has on job creation. The governors noted above are looking to completely eliminate over 150 special exemptions from taxes. This means unisex hair parlors, artwork, fishing boats, and other shop industries seeking immediate expansion upon exemption. Governors are looking at swapping from income tax regimes to consumption tax, taking note of prominent conservative economists like Milton Friedman, who for decades taught, wrote, and spoke of a socialist agenda intrinsic to confiscatory taxation that makes people dependent on government. For these and other economists, taxation on personal income sustains enormous harm simply because it's a penalty on savings, investment, and labor, the very sine qua non for wealth creation. By contrast, sales tax hits the results of wealth creation. Do the math or watch the migration.

States that have no income tax have far more stable revenue growth; while blue model states like Connecticut, New York, and California depend on the top 1 percent of earners for nearly 50 percent of state revenue. This model of taxation increases destabilizing swings in revenue collection. Socialists that dominate the Democratic Party's progressive agenda erroneously note that any tax swap to consumption is regressive. Mull that one over for a minute. To meet this onslaught of propaganda, many Republican governors are countering with bills exempting medicine, food, and utilities from sales tax while providing rebates to low-income families.

The bloom is off the rose for blue state tax and spend regimes. It's time that Connecticut's political class stop extracting from our most productive members to satisfy the political agenda of Harford's socialists.

State Pension Blow because of the Failed Liberal Policies

If you're a baby boomer, you're most likely looking at locations that are inexpensive. Given Connecticut's massive net loss of working population, Hartford's governing political class needs to consider its massive pension liabilities. Why? Because Hartford's progressive ideologues permanently threaten the state's fiscal health. Connecticut is sitting on a massive unwarranted pension crisis. No amount of tinkering with bookkeeping can surmount this challenge.

Blame is given to Connecticut's governing class for punting to capital markets in the hope of securing an annual 8 percent rate of return. That made sense before the crash. Now with Treasuries paying more after the demise of zero-interest-rate policy (ZIRP) coupled to dollar appreciation from global capital flows; this mix of appreciation and automatic increases in cost of living adjustments paves the way for a collapse of state pensions. A renegotiation of union contracts may be needed to stem the collapse.

The years 2013 to 2015 saw San Bernardino and Stockton, California, run the liberal playbook on any future collapse. The limousine liberals sought protection from bankruptcy only to be reminded that federal law trumps parochial state law. Their reasoning was state sovereignty. The second round saw this identical liberal class from California seek federal guarantee of its pension liability from Congress. Remember, too big to fail? Now the entire liberal political class throughout the union sought protection from its own profligate state spending. Both initiatives failed because federal courts cited Article VI of the US Constitution reserving federal law as supreme.

For those hardworking people wanting to know what happened to their biweekly contributions should look no further than annual spending. State pension funds are only minimally funded; the rest is spent on the discretion of Connecticut's political class favoring crony capitalism.

Deficits Don't Matter

When Reagan said that, he was referring to a reality that underwrote the monetarist achievement before the Great Moderation or the Greenspan Put—namely, a closed economy and fixed debt ratios. That reality is history. We now live in an era of open competition, global capital flows, floating exchange rates, and unlimited financialization of the economy. Reagan implicitly understood that deficits don't matter in an age of globalization, low union membership, massive productivity gains, new technologies, tax reform, and growth without inflation. So yes, fiscal and monetary environments matter.

Any comparison to today's progressive blowout minimizes the 1980s Reagan deficit; the progressive comparison to cite Reagan is unwarranted. That's because the true cost of government is the amount it spends, not borrows. The late, great Milton Friedman was fond of saying that government's current budget should be cut by 50 percent while running larger deficits. Today's progressive wing of the Democratic Party, prior to Speaker Ryan, increased the budget annually and financed its spending with continuing resolutions (IOUs). What's the strategy of the party of tax and spend? Democratic progressives view all this new debt creation as a way of forcing a permanently higher tax base on a dwindling demographic trend line. The liberal grand strategy is to use an accidentally large congressional majority passing new unfunded entitlements that explode in years to come. The result: higher tax rates across the board.

Reagan's deficits averaged about 20 percent of our current deficits. But remember how we got there and the dividend we received. The 1980s federal deficit financed the end of the Cold War through military buildup leading to a nearly thirty-year economic boom that ended stagflation. Today's progressives have exhausted the very formal economic and military institutions that served US interests in previous administrations. Borrowing and taxing to merely secure social gains has made America poorer.

So where is the GOP in all this mix? Well, numbers-wise, the GOP is trending upward. Republicans enjoy large margins in the House of Representatives joined to significant newly minted majorities in both statehouses as well as a deep, broad, diversified presidential pool. Not bad for sitting on the sidelines for eight years.

Truth be told, the Democratic Party is tired and worn worse given its near collapse of foreign policy traction. Ditto for its hidebound media handmaidens. They no longer enjoy unrivaled access to citizens. It's really all embodied in Nielson ratings. They've plummeted, and the corporate suits in C-Suite are lost because of it. But their turn is coming once President Obama leaves the stage and the motley patchwork of cronyism begins to eat each other. For Dems, without possessing the executive seat of government, the fault lines of the party for government will turn into deadly chasms. Remember Chambers and his Trotsky elk? No one spews invective and vitriol better than spurned progressives. The mistake was twofold. During Obama's tenure, progressive liberals became intoxicated with the fantasy of power. Only secondly did they discover what every fool in Washington knows politics only pretends to lead. Its role has always been recursive.

How We Got Here

When pundits across the nation begin eulogizing Obama's tenure, we need to remind ourselves how we got here, for 2016 needs to be a year of Democratic reckoning. Beginning in 2008, a Democratic senate class gave both Obama and Pelosi the desperately needed sixty-vote supermajority, passing pent-up generational health-care reform. Wait, it gets better. Every single one of those politicos now rejects Obamacare without ever having to defend such policy sentiment on the chamber floor. How about that? Remember how Alaskan Senator Ted Stevens was beaten by upstart Begich with a vote tally of barely 0.9 percent, only to have exculpatory evidence found favoring the incumbent Republican US senator. Remember Minnesota's Al Franken, who became Obama's sixtieth vote for Obamacare. That happened because of a strong-armed legal challenge for a vote recount tallying an additional 312 votes favoring neophyte Franken. We can count New Hampshire's Jeanne Shaheen, another Obamacare neophyte reluctantly defending her record while calling for exemptions amid the heath-care rollout. Let's not forget Mark Udall of Colorado, North Carolina's Kay Hagan, Arkansas's Mark Pryor, or Louisiana's Mary Landrieu. Every single one of them owns the Obamacare blowout. And each of them talks of reform or exemption without ever having to defend such policy on the chamber floor. Why? Because according to the Wyoming senator John Barrasso, Mr. Reid's amendment blockade is monolithic, having blocked 1,105 Republican senate amendments and 847 Democratic amendments. Nevada's senator has blocked every single US senate amendment but nineteen during Obama's tenure. If you ask anyone following the skullduggery, they'll note the comeuppance in 2016. That's if the GOP can stick together. A small note on historical, presidential electoral ratios is needed.

From 1992 to 2012, the Democratic Party won four of the last six presidential elections. Preceding that ratio, the GOP won five of the six presidential elections between 1968 and 1988. Those historical ratios break down given the myriad challenges presented to both races beginning in 2014. No amount of historical analogy can build symmetry given the fragmented nature of our candidacies and voting demography. To date, between 1994 and 2012, the Democratic Party has failed to win a majority in the House in eight of last ten elections. That puts into relief the dominant majority status they enjoyed from 1954 to 1992, winning twenty elections consecutively. The fiscal and demographic trends no longer fortify a Democratic ascendancy. To believe so is to endorse a backward-looking paradigm.

In its nearly 160-year history, the GOP has managed to assemble majorities favoring white Northern Protestants. However, as of this writing, the progressives have abandoned wide swaths of social demography, favoring urbanization instead. Today's Democratic Party isn't monolithic; it is riddled throughout with damaging paradoxes easily surmounted. Remember the 1 percent advantage delivered to Obama's presidency in 2012? It came from the Upper Midwest. But those margins are dangerously thin given the challenges America faces. Opposition to the Keystone XL pipeline, along with hostility to fracking, has damaged Democratic appeal in historical strongholds. Just ask anyone living in upstate New York. While damaging indigenous Democratic appeals in regions historically favorable to Democrats, they've abandoned entire manufacturing geographies. Progressives have delivered into the GOP large swaths of coal territory from Western Pennsylvania, moving south to Tennessee, including Texas and Arkansas. Beginning in Virginia, the South has been abandoned by the Democratic Party.

Not Your Dad's Democratic Party

Human beings are by nature sentimental, even archaic in their vision of time, change, and governing institutions. Prior to the arrival of digital technology, the relation among people was still modified by stalwart social institutions that served the interests of propriety. With the arrival of digital technology, we've welcomed the radicalization of autonomy, something that nature itself abhors.

An identical process is at work within the Democratic Party. Held together by their need to be the party for big government, they resemble the unassimilated, the deracinated. Uprooted without self-discipline, they simply cannot coalesce without strong centripetal force, molding direction while denying intrinsic worth. It wasn't always this way, for the party of Truman, Kennedy, and Dean Acheson had strong intellectual pedigree.

What happened?

It is safe to say that Lord Acton's dictum that absolute power corrupts held true for baby boomer leadership, for the ideas that animate Democratic polity are identical to fascist ideals. They simply became intoxicated with the fantasy of power, corrupting both the vision and their hold on policy implementation.

Historically the transformative presidency of Reagan is paradigmatic, for he brought forth an unalloyed skepticism about government while unleashing the growth of civil society embodied in economic growth and new technologies. The contrast with Obama is stark, for smart liberalism has no time to acknowledge the realities of bureaucratic inefficiencies. Remember, work expands to fulfill the time.

Private sector–working Americans know that only death itself eradicates federal job security. Redundancies, even negligence and incompetence, all have their place, if only because the ethos of the Democratic Party is that government alone should provide. Witness the near-death spiral that would have tanked most administrations during Obama's tenure. We've witnessed malfeasance and incorrigible skullduggery at Veterans Affairs, horrifying incompetence at IRS, Justice, and Health and Human Services. With Marx and the Socialists, there remained one tactic that could never be acknowledged nor reformed—the end justifies the means.

The Party of Growth

The election of 2014 saw an opening in growth that has gone unnoticed by dominant media—namely, that the GOP was poised to take control of both the House while gaining members in the Senate. This trend only reflects an uncouth realism neatly neglected in prominent media. The GOP is gaining on Obama and his progressive elk. From statehouses to governorships, the progressive wing of the current liberal establishment isn't holding its own anymore, and it is reflected in rising employment trends. Let's face it, working citizens are voting with both mouths and feet. A new confidence is brewing, and it is only found in acknowledging that corollary—the GOP stands for growth; progressives stand for welfare. The lifting of the Washington pall has begun.

The psychological effect of this public change in attitude should not be underrated. It means something very dangerous to contemporary progressives: The old Keynesian institutions that drove employment and growth don't respond anymore. Just ask any fed governor.

American businesses have hunkered down since 2008. Even with rising asset prices, soaring capital flows, and zero interest rates, the economy isn't growing with cash transfers. What explains the growth immediately before and after the 2014 election is quite simple. The pushback has begun.

The litany of imposition on US growth has been staggering. From the 2007 energy bill, Dodd-Frank, Obamacare, burdens on fossil fuels, coal, and governing by regulation continues apace. The GOP has presented alternatives that speak to the possibility of policy-led growth in the repeal or reform of the tax code, ease of burdensome regulations, health-care reform, and removal of barriers to job creation in permissive capital formation. November spoke clearly. The challenge of labor force participation rate is permanent without tax and labor reform. However, as November demonstrated, the self-destructive policy of progressive transfers has met the realism of an informed citizenry.

In late 2014, immediately before the election, the Tax Foundation released its State Business Tax Climate Index; the US ranks number 32—dismal. Launching a new International Tax Competitiveness Index, the Foundation seeks to measure the extent to which a nation's tax system adheres to two principles of fairness, competitiveness, and neutrality.

A competitive tax code isn't punitive, for it seeks to advance the capital, equity formation of its citizens. It can only achieve that if it advances the net remunerative gain across social classes. Notice the implicit need to safeguard the primacy of civil society. Because capital is mobile, high taxation drives investment out of high tax localities, leading to volatile swings in government revenue. The neutrality of the revenue advances gains with few distortions. Meaning the regime of taxation does not favor consumption over savings that happens with capital gains tax, estate tax. Both are hallmarks of progressive socialist regimes. The political arbitrage permitted by our current progressive system is unwarranted, for it prevents capital, equity formation while misallocating during the promotion of distortions. The US was ranked 32 out of 34 industrialized nation-states. Wait, the news gets better.

Having the United States possessing the world's highest corporate tax rate of 39 percent coupled to repatriation positions that of the US as a socialist regime. How? If you measure the US against the world's 190 countries, the US fairs worse. KPMG is an accounting firm ranking nations in a corporate tax table; the US leads one nation from last place, United Arab Emirates, which taxes at a 55 percent rate. The US is second to last place—pathetic. With repatriation, the US is in last place. Please note that Norway, Sweden, and Finland, with their exceedingly high-priced social safety nets, ranks in the top 20 in the KPMG ranking. Go figure.

Speaker Ryan and Reform of Congress

Conservative talk radio never did acknowledge how Speaker Ryan envisions decentralizing congressional assignments reflecting a federalist view of congressional leadership. Gone is the overt centralizing drive for bill origination out of the speaker's office. Bills will now originate from decentralized positions. This is the original view from the framers, and it puts Ryan and his party on offense. For those waiting to see how best to join the fray, they need to know that decentralized committee work will reflect the intellectual formation of those in charge. Historically Congress deferred to executive level bureaucrats originating from congressional committees. The result was a process driven by a variety of outside interests gaming an unwieldy process. The result is spending increases.

Technical fixes to a problem of overt centralization has been on display for decades. Remember the Gramm-Rudman-Hollings Reform in 1985? Wait, there was another in Gramm-Rudman II in '87. Like bad movie sequels, we even had pay-as-you-go throughout the 1990s. That morphed into supercommittees in 2011 and finally to sequester in 2012. The origin of the problem is an unwillingness for the Democratic Party to acknowledge limits to its governing. That's what budgets do; they acknowledge priorities and set limits implicitly, acknowledging the role civil society has in our Constitutional Republic. All this was denied during Obama's tenure, favoring continuing resolutions that gave open-ended fiscal commitments to government spending.

How best to begin the reform?

Decentralizing the bill origination process to committees for up-and-down votes in Congress is best. Omnibus bills should be ruled out with congressional leadership demanding roll calls on various individual bills. This should be done annually, providing continuity, order, and some resemblance of strategic priorities. Why will it work? No member of Congress wants to concede spending priorities to the president. Both chambers will work harder, resisting the self-aggrandizing that characterizes dysfunctional leadership, and minority party members still prefer having authority over their own spending priorities than relinquishing that authority.

Beginning in the House, regular order with bill origination decentralized from committee assignments.

And what of the Senate?

The senator from Nevada, Harry Reid, has shut down the Senate throughout Obama's tenure. The twin pillars of open debate and amendment are gone. To repair the institutional damage, the states themselves must restore the original constitutional relationship between themselves and the federal government. It's called federalism. As of today, US senators are freelancers. They do not embody, nor fortify, any constitutional relation because they aren't elected by state senate houses representing state interests. They simply represent themselves. What today's senators don't understand is that the Senate's procedural safeguards exist to protect liberty in equality, not individual senators. Another archaic procedural tool used by this chamber is the filibuster. This is a parliamentary procedural tool used to embarrass a dominant majority. By relinquishing this nuclear option forbidding filibusters, Harry Reid's party believes it can sustain adversarial media coverage when Republicans no longer advance parliamentary procedural tools in a Constitutional Republic.

Reforming the Senate would involve the following: Have state senate chambers elect US senators restoring constitutional order, regular order with bill origination in committee only, real deliberation in chamber with robust amendment procedures, finally, a longer work week.

Gas Taxes and Profligate Spending

The chief political reason for devaluation of currency is to better manage public finances. Politicians of both classes ignore the social impact of progressive taxation. Given the geopolitical state of the world, capital inflows continue to feed the Treasury, with many sovereign wealth funds and other transnational corporations, pensions, and foreign central banks using our capital markets to fund enterprises and equity positions, so it should surprise no one that Keynesian ideologues inside the GOP voted in January 2015 to raise the gas tax—the first raise in two decades.

It's a difficult truth to handle, but both dominant political classes ignore what is plain to any workingman or woman; the government uses its citizens to fund unsustainable social programs. The raiding of gas treasury is no different. Congress hates dollar appreciation; they love inflated currencies. With appreciation of the dollar, congressional expenditures have gotten expensive, so bipartisan lunacy gave us 18.4¢-per-gallon hike, even when gas prices overall have fallen more than 40 percent on average since 2014. Did you catch the propaganda? Congress will invest the windfall. Catch the logic: GOP members voted to raise the price of gas to offset discretionary income gains from cheaper gas. The gas tax, plus a 24.4¢ tax on diesel, with other excise taxes, finances a bankrupt Highway Trust Fund. You see, the HTF proceeds from the 1956 three-cent tax built the highway system that simulated American advance to Berlin under Eisenhower. However, beginning in 2008, federal HTF spending has grown faster than revenues with congressional cash transfers from general revenues making up the difference totaling

$54 billion. Covering future HTF obligations and managing deficits requires taxation. Absolutely no mention is given to exorbitant state contracts and other contractual subsidies driving expenditures in state-subsidized budgets. Keynesians ignore one side of the ledger to advance the other. They ignore advances in technology with more efficient cars or cheaper materials. No thinking is given to advances in domestic oil production and refining, assisting in cheaper asphalt. For Keynesians, the arc of history only bends one way.

Since the 1990s, the HTF abandoned its original user pay principle, favoring direct subsidization of mass transit. Drivers now see nearly 25 percent of their gas tax shifted over to ferries, sidewalks, bike lanes, hiking trails, urban planning, and landscaping. This occurs nationwide. Remember the bridge to nowhere? We've got one in every town.

The math is quite straightforward: If you use the HTF for highways, it's solvent, but then other streams of rent seeking go unattended. That's what really drives the gas hike. Simply put, the manufactured crisis is proportionally related to how monies are spent.

Regulation as Regulatory Capture

The scandal inherent in excessive uncritical liberal acceptance of government regulation needs to be exposed for what it is—progressive governments' punitive expedition to shatter any rival hegemony outside politics. Want to know where all the militant collectivists went after the end of the Cold War? They went to work for monolithic, unaccountable bureaucracies. The dirty secret isn't easy to disguise anymore given the dismal economic performance of team Obama post-2008. Their idea in excessively misplaced confidence in V-shaped recoveries can never accept a premise pointing to monetarist policy achievement. Better to speak in refrains about penumbras and arcs of history bending, for the passive voice embodies the liberal charlatan at his or her best. Enter Dr. George Stigler.

Some four decade ago, long before winning the Nobel Prize, George Stigler sought to study the impact regulations have on economies. It's staggering. Let's go through his landmark study marking him for a Nobel in economics.

The 1971 Bell Journal of Economics and Management Science published an essay titled "The Theory of Economic Regulation." The essay purports to reveal a staggering truth secretly pursued by every militant collectivist—namely, that regulations are acquired by industries exclusively for their benefit. Mull that one over for a minute. For it points to conflicts of interest that the rule of law is supposed to prevent; the inevitability of regulatory capture requires statutory clarity so as to prevent gaming by the most influential firms and their captured bureaucracies. Want to end the political rent seeking that dominates Washington, DC? Legislate a flat tax and every lobbyist is unemployed. Here's one closer to home. Remember Timothy Geithner's time at the New York Federal Reserve. While working for the US Federal Reserve, he permitted Citigroup to hold $1.2 trillion in bonds, including more than $600 million of mortgage-backed (related) securities, in off-balance-sheet vehicles immediately before the financial crisis. Ditto for Treasuries Jack Lew at Citigroup, now treasury secretary.

To end the gaming, the cheerleading and partisan rancor of rent seeking just repeal Dodd-Frank and Basel Rules replacing them with simpler compliance regimes, say equity-to-asset ratios of 10 percent. How about bringing back the relevancy of bankruptcy for resolution instead of operating extra judicially through politically allocated appointees that can be manipulated. The cynicism is nearly bottomless. Nearly. For leadership will end this nonsense, favoring an operating ethos of a true republic, one that embraces liberty in equality, not farce.

By the way, Dr. Charles Calomiri's idea tackling the political rent seeking that makes banks easily fragile and susceptible to extreme volatility by automatically converting portions of bank debt into equity when specific portfolio components fall below value was a significant policy development. Washington admonished Dr. Calomiri's plan because it wiped out the very political manipulation that Washington wants in banks. Remember, only in militant collectivist societies can authority become unlimited. We should anticipate monolithic, unaccountable government departments to begin exercising eminent domain over numerous spheres of citizens' lives. Remember Detroit bondholders and AIG?

The African American Black Vote

It is clear to anyone more than a few decades old that progressives take the African American vote for granted. Consider some basic economics.

In 2008, the unemployment rate was 12.7 percent for African Americans. It was 7.1 percent for whites. In January, four years after Obama's first term, the number grew to 13.8 percent. The gap between African Americans and whites is widened. Today, the number is still double that of white unemployment. If you consider the labor participation rate, this measures a share of the working age population that is employed. It isn't any better because the last time African American's suffered this trend was 1978. The black labor force participation rate is 61.7 percent. Dismally low.

Black poverty rates aren't any better either. The number remains stuck at 27.2 percent; for whites, it's 14.5 percent.

Median household incomes have fallen for nearly every single working American under this president. Median black household incomes fell to $34,598 in late 2013; white households dropped to $58,270 from over $62,000. The numbers do not portray an executive interested in alleviating black poverty. How is it that black median household income was merely 61 percent of whites? Instead of policy traction, permanent campaigning was the tool applied in the solicitation of grievance for the purpose of contrived fear and repression.

How did we arrive here? The answer is really quite simple. The appeal to racial solidarity is performed because the Democratic Party cannot make the case based on empirical results. The sad truth is that the Democratic Party has abandoned African Americans, favoring instead suburban whites.

The Fed's Foul Mouth Denial

The institutions that working American citizens ought to be angry with are the US Federal Reserve and Treasury, for currency manipulation works both ways and hasn't been the sole responsibility of nefarious Chinese communists. The truth is far more prosaic. We have our own indigenous Communist Party here in the United States. However, both the Federal Reserve and Treasury are the primary institutions that have contrived to accommodate an overt socialist social order chiefly through denial. Given Yellen's incredulous denials during house testimony about auditing the Federal Reserve by the government accountability office (GAO), we expect her unwillingness to confront the political consequences of a reckoning to underwrite her denial. The ground has shifted under her feet, and Yellen is struggling to adhere to some resemblance of contrived order. Nevertheless, the monetarist experiment of baseline money growth fit several philosophical and historical postulates at the Fed. Those are gone now. And she's struggling to find her new footing in a political order that animates lost fed independence, a postulate that only worked when there was affinity between the Democratic dominant political majority in Congress and Treasury. That contrived order was impossible to hold to any realist reckoning given the policy wiles of Washington. Let's dive a bit deeper into the monetary morass.

The institutionalized impact of a complete financial meltdown inaugurated by lowering mandating underwriting standards is on display for all to see—namely, a politicized Federal Reserve. Immediately before 2016, Chairman Yellen wanted to get off the zero-bound, zero-interest-rate policy (ZIRP) to inaugurate normalizing monetary relations. Why? Because this once august body is completely exhausted at the hands of accommodating a failed political class bent on monetary experimentation. Throughout the Obama administration, working Americans have witnessed very large swings in exchange rates, rapid capital outflows and inflows with unprecedented volatility. Most economies just couldn't keep up with the movements of globally connected central bankers whose real job is maintenance of the cost of money. These rapid volatile trends damaged businesses models and disrupted businesses cycles, instead favoring politically connected clients. Savors, working mothers, and those on fixed income got destroyed. Such are the consequences from politically mispriced credit or capital. All to the detriment of an institution that favored "independence."

The vast majority of those monetary exertions were ultimately at the service of institutionalized political fragility—the banks, whose structure is regulated to accommodate dominant political majorities, not bondholders. As the late, great Ann Schwartz revealed to the Wall Street Journal editorial board in 2012, the great banking crisis was not the result of insufficient liquidity, but a capitalization problem.

Sheeple and Group Think

The most harmful effect of not having a V-shaped recovery is moral and intellectual. Perhaps the gnomes at central banks can spend a little time surveying problems with their monetary transmission channels or, better yet, an unwanted recognition that interest rates and demand are now permanently disjointed. If so, they better dump Keynes and look to classical monetarists who saw firsthand what a central bank can and cannot do, something a Fabian resists.

The US Federal Reserve was only interested in assisting the political class in Washington, not the American people. Let me explain. ZIRP (zero-interest-rate policy) was all about the maintenance of public finance. It was sold, advertised to the public as an elixir without ever having examined the role digital technology has on our society or the central banks transmission channels. ZIRP was sold to the working American as a fix to our broken economy. It failed. Why? Because the thought behind the policy is wrong. It was Keynesian, meaning it was backward looking. The Keynesian gnomes thought that investment (borrowing) is inversely related to interest rates. But throughout our recovery, American citizens and business formation was stuck at historic lows with very little capital formation. Why did our economy remain sluggish with ZIRP? The answer is found by reversing the logic of the premise. Why? Because politics matters. Investment is inversely proportional to the taxation of capital and the growth of the Federal Register. But don't ask that of central bankers who never ran a business or struggled to make payroll.

There's a reason why the dismal science was once called political economy.

What Israel Teaches: Ben-Gurion's Aliya

Thomas Carlyle's overly weaned motif that history is boiled down to great men is in need of revision; for how does one make sense of Israel? When Irving Kristol arrived in Jerusalem to deliver a lecture titled "On The Political Stupidity of the Jews," many pondered the relevancy of his chosen topic. Like Richard Feynman's infamous "There's Plenty of Room at the Bottom" lecture, both faculty, administration, and students ignored it for thinking its application severely parochial. In Feynman's case, the idea was extreme (digital, atomic) miniaturization; in realty, his audience thought his chosen topic referred to adjunct teaching. Both scored resoundingly well in foresight. Given the depth of our current domestic and foreign challenges, I would mine the character of these men and their distinct achievements to discern how best to meet our present challenges. For Kristol, the solution to Israeli identity and national trajectory lay in its ability to absorb and apply lessons from Thucydides on the realities of power; from Adam Smith, on the intrinsically ethical nature of economic liberty; from Edmund Burke, an ability to discern opposing trends between politics and irreconcilable domestic political tradition(s); finally, from Tocqueville, on the need to discern the satanic, genocidal trends that lay inert in democratic polities.

However, it remains to be mined how Jewish tradition, especially its Roman and Greek challenge spoke to Jewish polity about identity, mission, and foreign threats. That ruse continues, albeit differently today. Somewhere deep in Ukrainian, Lithuanian, or Polish Eastern European philosophical tradition lie keys yet to be discerned on how best Jewish religious identity can surmount the social challenge of modernity. The truth is difficult to say, but rabbinic Judaism has had very little to offer those seeking to surmount the political crisis that envelopes Israel post Oslo Accord.

Israel today flourishes.

It has survived the lie, animating entire fiefdoms at State Department and Islamic civilization at large—namely, that peace will be achieved if Israel conceded ground favorable to Arab proxies: Palestinians. It has now come to pass.

The daily knifings around the Temple Mount in Old Jerusalem reveal a deeply troubling mind-set, one that has finally turned inward and retreated from the only position favorable to Arab self-determination—namely, politics. Hundreds of millions of dollars gone, Abbas and his unelected henchmen straddle an irreconcilable reality; it's over, and the Jews after Oslo have moved on toward building an indigenous Israeli political tradition, a reinvigorated Jewish nationalism, one alloyed outside rabbinic sources. What has Abbas built? Even with global patronage, Palestinians never built institutions necessary for a peaceful state. No rule of law, no room for civil society and its little platoons (the term is Burkes), and no means to measure public sentiment as electoral. Under these circumstances, the notion of a two-state solution has become delusional.

What does all this mean? It means that Israel, alone in an Islamic neighborhood, must continue to build formal alliances with those on its periphery. It means preemptive war. It means cleaning up the neighborhood. In a word: leadership. While it sells desalinization plants to Riyadh, builds envious world-class air defense systems, and runs the world's best educational facilities for Arab Israelis to enjoy, it lives on each day fortifying Reagan's polite admonition: Peace through strength.

The Demographic Challenges of Merkel's Syrian Moment

A new Götterdämmerung is taking shape within Germany, and it is the single most significant challenge to Germany since the defeat of corporal Hitler. Demographic implosion. The challenge of modernity is low fertility, and it's playing out in Teutonic and Slavic Eurasian heartlands, favoring a return to previous political maelstroms that characterized the twentieth century. Make no mistake; Merkel's advisors have made a Keynesian bet favorable to future constituencies, for her idea of clemency welcoming Syrian refugees isn't divorced from her Machiavellian grasp of contemporary demographic trends. She's decided to build a new constituency. We wait the returns.

For those who knew utopian communism, her decision isn't out of line with rational calculation. She misplaces her confidence in believing that government policy can build what civil society holds and retains. Germany remained the vortex of international relations since the late nineteenth century. It ended badly for them with defeat and total collapse in '47. Her country divided between ideological loyalties with demographic dispersions, political disintegration, economic dislocation, and seemingly permanent social alienation. The psychological oppression born within geography had never found resolution.

Until 1989. Then the deluge.

Those who survived the awakening, the near physical annihilation, flourished. Her advisors gave her scenarios. All of them built on the false premise of modernity.

Merkel's Germany has turned its back on utopian democratic socialism. It now resides within a postnational identity. Having moved beyond parochial identity, having deliberately embraced the weakening, the fraying of religious and cultural norms underwriting Germania, she's opened her borders in the hope that her defensive posture can hide what realists know. She's welcoming and becoming a polite nihilism. Having abandoned national identity for the thin vice of unalloyed liberty in moral relativism, she will build a Germania unaccustomed to the wiles of a virulent Eurabia. With religious and ethical norms underwriting Teutonic ideals withered and gone, Eurabic-Germania will display cool detachment identical to young Western progressives; empty, self-satisfied, and lacking purpose, they surrender the key to growth: self-determination. Under the threat of a militant Eurabia tied to genocidal philosophies of immanence, Germania will fold, easily. Remember, we've been here before.

Meanwhile other nations, having gone through identical catastrophe's like Poland, will find the challenge of Eurabia a difficult means to encounter, but they will not yield to an encroaching militancy. Surrounded by secular tyrannies and religious extremists in open borders identical to the times of ruling Khans, entire countries will face annihilation, except those who didn't eschew the ethical, theological foundations of society.

The irreconcilable challenge that imminent statesmen must confront at the beginning of the twenty-first century is daunting: How best to enunciate and defend the moral foundations of society.

The Great War, High Modernism, and Modern Life

If the novel fell out of Gogol's "Overcoat," then modernity, in all is permutations, arrived in full grandeur, sprung from the Danubian basin. Vienna and nodes hidden throughout the Austrian–Hungarian Empire remain the sole repository to understand how we arrived at a disintegrating civilization. The Somme, Marne, Thomas Mann, and Keynes all have their cultural antecedents alongside Sarajevo. We must mine them to discern the trends that animate contemporary inversions of our moral order.

The seductive beauties of the summer of 1914, well told in Barbara Tuchman's The Proud Tower, obscures more than reveals. The social, political stability embodied in consanguine monarchies from London to the Eurasian plain seemed correlative to European stability. But brewing deep within the vortex of this objective balminess were revolutionaries committed to overthrowing the very social order that sustained them. We've forgotten Bismarck's admonition that one day, some damned fool would unleash a conflagration from the Balkans. And so the war came.

The fashionable nihilism of Russia's intelligentsia had a long home in the geography of Germania. Helmuth von Moltke, presiding as chief of staff to the Prussian Hohenzollern Empire, opined privately in his diary that he welcomed a world war, for it would lie to waste, all of Christendom, leaving Germany alone in its mortal conflict with Russia. The only clear-eyed realist was London's Sir Edward Grey, the esteemed foreign secretary. He took the measure of England's enemy and found his own nation wanting. He alone, like Churchill, foresaw that a world war would end the social order.

When September arrived in 1915, the French, British, and German soldiers would slaughter each other to man; a million casualties in one week alone. The butchery that became trench warfare in an age of total war began. It fortified nothing. It unleashed a world of abstractions that continue to dominate even a mercantile world like ours today. The West has known nihilism.

The dilemma that haunted the protagonists was simple enough. The war was fought to decide a moral, an intellectual enterprise. Each protagonist sought to compel a parochial resolution to a problem confined to international politics—the mastery of Europe—but under the banner of what faith? You see, empire alone cannot account for the revolution in sensibility that became high modernism, nor can any account from competing empires really distill the Great War, for the revolutionaries that arrived when Empire exhausted itself amounted to a total crisis of morality. This crisis found resolution in the statecraft of the 1980s, but the war itself, and high modernity with it, precipitated, aggravated a permanent crisis in Western cultural, political life that continues today. Narcissism and the tribal night had both progeny and patrimony.

The Great War was fought by England to preserve a world, a culture of imperialism that defined the empire. Germania fought to bring down that very world. The malignant fantasies of fin-de-siè-cle Weimar, Vienna, or Bonn have their beginning in the hothouse atmospherics of militant sentimentality embracing guilt as a formal instrument of policy. Grievance begins in Vienna, and a serially pathological art student inconsolable from defeat begins the journey to ratify his rage. That sentimentality of rage would scale itself, becoming a burgeoning totalitarianism. In a word, Palestine.

The inversion of our inherited moral order has large historical antecedents in today's political environment of homosexual unions, in the nomenclature of positivist thought in law divorced from natural right and in international relations as witnessed throughout Islamic civilization.

It didn't begin with America.

When Dr. Modris Eksteins wrote Rites of Spring, he cited an extraordinary revolting precipice embodying the malevolent deployment of politicized rage. In the final days of World War II, the Russian were closing in on Berlin before the Americans. The vast majority of the Nazi High Command evacuated themselves to Adolf Hitler's underground bunker. The date was May 1. Josef Goebbels injected his six children with morphine, and when they were unconscious, his dutiful wife and he crushed glass ampules of cyanide in their mouths. A few days before this incident, Goebbels's wife had written a farewell letter to her son, Harald Quandt, a son from a previous marriage. She wrote the following: "Our splendid concept is perishing and with it goes everything beautiful, admirable, noble, and good that I have known in my life. The world which will succeed the Fuhrer is not worth living in, and for this reason, I have brought the children here with me. They are too good for the life that will come after us... Harald, my dear, I give you the best that life has taught me—be true, true to yourself, true to mankind, true to your country, in every respect whatsoever."

The totalitarian belief in radical militant autonomy fortified and shaped from within philosophies of immanence was Germania. Now it is Islam, and only a confrontation with militant realism will resolve it.

The House of Saud: Endgame

It's ironic that we arrive at the hundredth anniversary of the demise of European Christian monarchy at a time when the last vestiges of archaic Islamic monarchies are engulfed in survival. The Saudis have bought, murdered, sold, lied, and prostrated themselves before superior foes; it is now ending. The closing of Islamic rule from encirclement will be very nasty, and Obama's realism is to thank for pushing policies whose indirect impact would seal the fate of Riyadh.

Panic has set in as we witness the beheadings of forty-seven Shiite terrorists who've been imprisoned in Saudi Arabia for decades. With the execution of the prominent Shiite cleric Nemer al-Nemer, charged with capital crimes for leading an uprising in Arabia's heavily Shiite-dominated eastern province including Bahrain, the Saudi pursuit of scorched-earth policy comes on the heels of losing Yemen.

Witnessing Iranian encirclement after the US abandoned both Egypt to the Muslim Brotherhood while pursuing Iranian détente proved to Riyadh that the Americans are gone. Saudi Arabia's problems grow at an alarming rate, and it cannot address them. By any reckoning, the House of Saud is folding before us.

Unable to implement counterinsurgency doctrine throughout its southern perimeter in Yemen, abandoned by its most trusted source for land engagement (the Pakistani's), disturbing subsidies-eating unsustainable deficits, and importing labor because its indigenous polity is subsidized in permanent welfare, the Saudis are facing domestic, international, and regional threats with minimum resources and dwindling industrial base. It now seeks to purchase nuclear material to build its own deterrent. Will Islamabad help?

The implosion of its market share to US fracking has been met with increased production at the expense of Putin's domestic agenda. It seeks to purchase desalinization plants from Jerusalem while ignoring the very policy needed to survive, a diversified political economy. Like all arcane specialists, the Saudis only flourish in artificially maintained environments. Now a Russian bear appears in its northern tier, and Istanbul isn't answering the beckoning from Riyadh. Will the Saudis seek to flank Moscow by turning to the Caucasus region moving north along the Volga? The House of Saud is both Machiavellian and Hobbesian. It will pay to devour the House of Muscovy.

The Saudis are very difficult allies, but the flailing has only begun.

The Syrian Bazaar

The implementation of policy requires a mind-set accustomed to moving velocities and magnitudes, not fixed relations. That is why the post–Cold War world is far better suited to someone familiar with ancient, medieval, or even eighteenth century diplomacy. Most protagonists possessed identical weaponry, only geography, weather, leadership, and few other intangibles shaped any decisive conflict.

The nonentry of American leadership in Syria portends badly for the Americans.

We've abandoned entire nation-states to the wiles of militant autocrats, whom we've calculated are better than the Islamic State, but this ignores our unwilling agency to shape events prior to 2015, when we had advantages useful for engagement. Because we've sat out this fight, we abrogated any regional influence. No one listens to us now nor fears us.

As of this writing (2016), US leadership applied to Syria will require executive policy engagement that the entire Obama administration is unwilling to learn, apply, nor assist in a regional proxy use to our interests. The sum zero struggle between Sunni and Shia proxies will dominate this region until Russia or Saudi Arabia succeeds or exits in exhaustion. As of now, both Muscovy and Riyadh will exhaust itself, leaving an emerging Iranian hegemony. The diplomatic push is leavened by idealist rhetoric fit for those unable to rule. Secretary of State John Kerry speaks of "inclusive, nonsectarian governance with free and fair elections." This isn't serious diplomacy, and it makes potential future US leadership look bad. Our abrogation signals weakness to NATO allies embroiled with an enraged Russia seeking expansion. Because we don't seek out Russian weakness, we give up that nature of our enterprise, effectively strengthening Russian advance. Our NATO allies haven't threatened Russia, leaving Putin's Baltic interior lines of supply and communication intact. Because our political leadership is unwilling to govern from realist assumptions of power, Russian natural gas pipelines through Ukraine into Germany linking Italy and France cannot be used against Putin. It means that Russian intervention throughout the Eastern Mediterranean is aiding Putin's political ambitions whose strategic purpose is to play spoiler to America's soft cop image.

The stakes in this game could easily have been stoked favorably to our interest if we had an engaged earlier with a stalwart executive heavily fortified by a state department committed to serving US interests.

The ambitions of millions throughout North Africa, Mesopotamia, and the Eastern Mediterranean would have been realized.

Why Trump Matters

When the northern Presbyterian Irishman Edmund Burke began writing Reflections on the Revolution in France, he was deeply engaged with George III Hanoverian court over outrageous claims of corruption. This should surprise no one, for immediately after the Tudor revolution, the British began an outstanding policy of tying down France (its main competitor and enemy in the new world), moving east long the Rhine. London wanted France permanently engaged deep in Germany's interior as a distraction from the new world. It worked, for a long while; then it collapsed. The source of England's best geopolitical triumph is too often sentimentalized. In reality it was graft that kept the social mores of England's foreign policy mechanics going. The blue water versus continental policy triumph cannot be separated from the contretemps of political life. It is the same today regarding the vested interests of modern bureaucratic life, especially when the mores of monolithic entities no longer possess the interests of the governed. Being a Constitutional Republic means that the form of the regime actually incorporates discrete passions of the union. Today, it doesn't. It cannot. And it remains to be seen how modern, unelected fiefdoms can sustain themselves when they are organized to govern in permanent opposition. Nixon understood this best before Watergate.

Since progressives actually remain the party of big government, it needs to be asked how this party as government can remain on the receiving end of government largess and favoritism if we are to continue being a Constitutional Republic. Where's the Republican ethos infused throughout Obama's cabinet? Where's the drive to incorporate ideological diversity, the sine qua none of progressive thought? It isn't there. Obeisance is enough. Our founders embodied perfect symmetry of diversity regarding political order and policy resolution. Madison himself always thought that government should remain outside the confines of public gratuity. Hamilton actually felt that the common good required the federal government to play a positivist role. His thinking resembles contemporary Asian economies that are governed by benevolent diktats. We should remember that even though Hamilton dominated throughout the nineteenth and twentieth century, it was permanently infused by Madison's regime. Today, throughout the United States and Europe, traditional political traditions that mitigated institutional collapse have permanently faltered.

A social, political revolution is brewing. Are they reading Tocqueville?

Europe's long, lost tradition of enlightened absolutism has returned, and this time, it isn't Gallic but Prussian, for Kant embodies the trend emerging throughout Europe as demonstrated in European supranational identity favoring transnational policies. The corruption of indigenous political institutions that historically favored protection against dominant majorities has eroded, favoring antidemocratic institutions. At stake aren't just democracy or democratic institutions but the impartial application of law itself. A few examples would suffice.

The fourteenth amendment's equal protection clause or the fallacious doctrine known as substantive due process are shaped from within a political philosophy of grievance that nullifies natural rights, favoring instead outcomes or rights resembling a pluralism that seeks the destruction of "E pluribus unum." Here, positive law operates inside a morally undifferentiated pluralism, a separation of ethics from ontology, rendering the proponents of union untenable. American progressives have summarily rejected the natural order as immutable, instead favoring nominalist neo-Kantian tendencies whereby language makes reality based on the application of pure reason. Having rejected natural law, American progressives endorsed a putative law of history, political development, economics, and arcs. They've replaced Locke with Hegel, adapting new social conditions to the mores of unhistorical, undefined sources right.

What has Trump taught? He's embodied the very mercantile ethos that rent Machiavelli and ruled the materialist West since antiquity. Yet Reagan's achievement was never mined outside the galvanizing heights of the Cold War. Truth be told, the West, under an American aegis, has yet to field a resolution to the spiritual, moral confines of domestic policy.

If anything, Trump has proved often enough that political institutions reflect the state of our culture.

Even still, contra Trump, the counterrevolution has begun.

An Industrial Base Built for the Long War and the Pax Americana

As each member of the Joint Chiefs of Staff began abandoning Bush, it became clear to Cheney and others close to him that America's war-fighting base had become an adult jobs program. The threat of having America's nuclear deterrent fold up was very frightening. The win delivered by Petraeus, Kagan, and others was a very near thing. The root of the problem isn't simple. And the solutions to addressing America's industrial fighting complex will not be resolved by tweaking Pentagon procurement ratios alone. The contours of this problem are revealed deep within the QDR (Quadrennial Defense Review Board), but nothing short of a monetarist revolution from the next American president can resolve this problem. Members of Congress's Armed Services Committee throughout 2016 are scheduled to resume addressing some budgetary dimensions to a problem that is truly insurmountable, for no American president should ever experience abandonment. Civil-Military relations in only for the hidebound, even still, the military industrial complex failed miserably in its mission in Iraq. That's because our leaders think of war as mechanized conflict. What happens when the enemy doesn't oblige? As General Westmoreland found, the concepts of mechanized statecraft can be mitigated by geography, fanaticism, and imaginative use of patience. In a phrase: militant humanism. This institutionalized failure and its reversal has historical antecedents—in Vietnam under General Abrams, with Lincoln under Grant, and Reagan's applied statecraft of counterinsurgency (COIN) doctrine throughout El Salvador and Guatemala in the 1980s.

The trend is familiar. But it must be said anyway. War is a business and a very sexy one. Careers aren't made performing the long, hard slog of conventional war to root out miscreants in far-off corners of the world.

Just ask anyone today in the Air Force or Navy. The Keynesian ideals that underwrite America's war machine are useless against Islamic fanaticism. Addressing this with wholesale monetarist reform of our entire military industrial complex, beginning with tax reform, is the only way forward. Why? Because the sources of renewal in this generational conflict cannot be found in the application of overt mass on the battlefield; the sources of renewal are civil, and the drive of executive statecraft is to open the tenants of our mercantile civilization, appealing to Islam's egalitarian premise and stealing the very social prestige that breeds the envy and discontent throughout the land of Arabia.

What can the late nineteenth and early twentieth century teach war planners and our future president about reforming our war complex? If we mine what Mao saw in his grasp of mechanized war, our military leaders will have a much better grasp of the limits of applied mass. COIN experts aren't wrong in their admonition that infantry will regain its prestige as the fulcrum of American engagement abroad. Nevertheless, the Germans rightly believe that history is the base of all military conflicts. The study of this base trains experience while teaching the art of command in difficult environments where the application of mechanized force becomes void. What infantry inculcates is the habit of acting correctly without having to think. The nineteenth- and twentieth-century military trinity of positional warfare embodied in preparation, mass, and impulsion have been refuted and replaced with deception, indirect attack, and strategic patience. Sun Tzu commands Westmoreland.

Throughout the nineteenth and early twentieth centuries, the active agents of imperialism were superior civilians that implicitly understood entire continents. Britain was known to advance political agents deep into the interior of Eurasia without communication or handling, for the matter of long-range strategic interests compelled them to use human intelligence to advance national interests. What these civilian agents procured was outstanding intelligence about the ideological nature of enemies and the sources and limits of particular regimes, something expensive bureaucracies cannot obtain. Throughout the Cold War, intelligence desks in London continued to apply civilians for the purpose of statecraft throughout the continent. These men and women were far better suited to the social geography of enemy terrain than bureaucracies. Ask our regional allies if the assigned CIA officer in Kabul, arriving a few days every month, has any handling on emerging trends. To the Islamic militants throughout Southwest Asia, we compel their drive to annihilate us. And just as England feared a continental coalition rising against her, Iranian agents throughout Latin America and Canada are encircling us.

That's because work expands to fulfill the time.

A Road Map: In Thanks to Dr. Allan Meltzer

Most academics never find a way toward high journalism. Dr. Allan Meltzer never had to give his unflinching admiration and support to Margaret Thatcher's monetarist charge before Scargill ate up her time and prestige. Let's not forget, it was he alone who fortified her spine in light of dominant Keynesians who sought to emasculate her in the Times of London. After speaking to Dr. Meltzer and witnessing her immediate affinity to Hayek's oeuvre, Meltzer affirmed in her that her political instincts were right. Like Reagan, her success cost her dearly; she only recovered long after the affair was over.

It fell to Dr. Allan Meltzer to do it again, this time with Congress's attempt to audit the Federal Reserve and implement a rule chosen by fed governors; the need to bring coherency to this entity has been long overdue. The chair of the Federal Reserve, Yale University's Dr. Janet Yellen, has learned a thing or two about optics from the Obama presidency. This partially explains why congressional leadership called on Dr. Meltzer to explain to this august body the need to form a rule, a framework that would help eliminate the very kabuki theatre characterizing exchanges between Congress and the Fed. Remember the old Soviet adage, "We pretend to work, they pretend to pay us." Exchanges between Treasury and the fed chair happen weekly without any oversight as to the policy goals, aims, and general overall political structure fielded between both agencies, agencies mandated to be managed by Congress. In light of the central role the Federal Reserve played in the financial crisis of 2008, Congress has sought to elicit from the Federal Reserve a self-prescribed rule or framework for affinity between Congress and the Fed. Yellen's testimony throughout the summer and early winter of 2015 demonstrated a fear unbecoming for someone as formidable as she. Clearly the ground has shifted under her and flailing in an otherwise obtuse role. Her polite lies and obfuscation yielded what Congress sought authorities outside the Fed to assist in assigning the Congressional Accountability Office a central role in auditing how the Federal Reserve arrives at discrete macroprudential policy.

The rules versus discretionary template that dominates television in its coverage of the Federal Reserve isn't helpful for two reasons. One, the medium of television isn't fit for the extreme abstractions of Keynesian thought. Two, neither template is sufficient. What's required is far more policy clarity Congress expects from the central bank. What Congress seeks is a defined objective that the Federal Reserve would apply to its policy machination. A rule not imposed by Congress. Milton Friedman and Anne Schwartz sought to have the governing members of the central bank remember the social and political impact the real bills doctrine had to fixed exchange rates; a terrible moralizing of Protestant ethics to a specific regime of currency evaluations and volatility. The result was the Great Depression. Nominal GDP has replaced monetarism in that Keynesians seem to have enshrined in Washington parlance the efficacy of spending. They, too, have embraced the very weapon used to defeat them.

What auditing the central bank achieved is a political consensus regarding how the central bank works. Its mandates are difficult to reconcile to reality. In fairness, the Federal Reserve has been burdened with irreconcilable policy objectives of maximum employment, price stability, and moderating long-term interest rates. Just how the central banks work out its role in achieving these competing roles is what Congress is seeking.

Thanks to Dr. Allan Meltzer, finding how to achieve another Great Moderation is in the making.

Moral Norms and the Created Order

Looking back on the statesmanship of Eastern or Central Europe immediately after the end of the Cold War reminds me of a significant insight that underwrites the superiority of the American political regime. The United States is a Constitutional Republic; we have fused two distinct capacities of the human mind that remained separated until the founding. They remained separated because the animating principle of European civilization was monarchy or the divine right. Until this was challenged by the discovery of the new world and its distinct social, political impact on Protestant mercantile sensibilities, a moral insight into political regimes, or social organization was not possible. European order and its most prominent critics were unable to speak of moral relations or compacts. Instead, they remained stymied in Cartesian or positivist thought regarding contracts. This terminology, reflective of European social order, never took hold in the Americas. This very conflict of senses and social order occurred immediately after the end of the Cold War in Poland, Czechoslovakia, Ukraine, and numerous other revolutions termed colored revolutions. The permanence or strength of the revolution remained proportional to the sources underwriting the dominant culture. Why? Because what shaped and propelled the revolutions to succeed in Central or Eastern Europe was the dominant role theology had as the distinct source of culture. The theological sources of culture shaped and brought to fruition a moral foundation toward liberty. "The shot heard 'round the world" caught on and grew. This is why globalization and the Arabic discontent are joined.

American secular culture, typically organized from within the dominant medium of television, a medium unfit to carry discrete abstract principles of literate thought, homogenized American perception to ignore deeper sources of our political regime. The narcosis of television never invites the interrogative.

A few prominent American thinkers like James Q. Wilson, Daniel Patrick Moynihan, Norman Podhoretz, and others were capable of discerning emerging political trends while criticizing Marxism and its indigenous permutations that rocked European thought for centuries. These distortions of thought never really found a home here in America. With Marxism, we have an oeuvre chiefly framed from within the social confines of organized machinery; deriding the created order as a fulcrum, it sought justification in having intellectual revolutionaries murder their way to the commanding heights of the nation-state. With Teutonic Nietzsche, we discern a tortured soul claiming how herds solidify the cult of romantic revolutionary leadership. Castro with Kraut.

All these so-called intellectual trends and their satanic political regimes embraced murder, sedition, and class war as the weapon of organization. Like today's contemporary progressives that run the Democratic Party, they seek the criminalization of political differences.

Eastern Europe's success in transitioning out from militant socialism cannot be separated from Christian ethics. An identical challenge animates contemporary militant secularism—how to reconcile social trends that seek permanent rupture of every natural bond whose origin is found in the created order.

What the founding ratified as a Constitutional Republic was a premise that ancient empires and different civilizations we're incapable of reconciling: human freedom and identity as an indissoluble reserve for the preservation of a gift—life.

A World Bequeathed

The disarmament promises in the Far East are falling apart. So is Mesopotamia and Persia. The single most significant development in global foreign affairs is the American threat deterrent, both nuclear and military. No other deployed asset manages threats and potential adversaries better than our armed forces, but the pace of contemporary proliferation is outpacing our capacities. The next president must field superior statecraft to confront, diminish, and wind down emerging threats. It will take an enormous amount of capital, both fiscal, moral, administrative, and intellectual to accomplish this feat.

A dangerous new era of proliferation is upon is. This time the newly emerging regimes possess dangerous political, theological veneers that attract domestic adherents to the West. The Cold War has precedents, yet the reach, depth, and pace of these nuclear break-outs makes previous templates of diplomatic calculation inadequate. We go on the offensive or we perish.

Globalization isn't the sole culprit fortifying the race to field nuclear advances. The American tax regime contributes as well. The mechanics and consequences of our own domestic social order for-tify the outward pace of global capital flows. Ditto for easy mobile technology, cheap labor, and open borders. All contribute to the retardation of American preeminence. We're simply not competing. To turn this around, the panoply of American statecraft must be employed by an executive willing to publicly expound and defend American interests that underwrite international order. As nuclear missile technology, delivery, and miniaturization outpace detection, the Americans remain the only hope of eliminating geopolitical vol-atility. Previous presidents did it. The next one must, or our threat deterrents diminish.

Diplomatically the next American president must consider the reform of the state. Having a permanently fractured instrument of diplomacy diminishes our capacities abroad. Just ask the Israelis and Saudis. The House of Saud has already began building nuclear facil-ities. A nuclear arms race has already begun in the heart of Islamic civilization, a society bred on political norms inconsistent with Judeo-Christian order. We may not be able to contain nor shape the contours of the geopolitical interests of foreign civilizations, but try we must.

As for the Far East, we really have only one hope. Missile tech-nology. South Korea, like Taiwan, has returned to the political camp of realism, and the United States must field THAAD or Terminal High Altitude Area Defense. It's Reagan's grown-up Star Wars. As of this writing, the communist regime in Beijing plies Seoul not to build this platform that would integrate American and Japanese missile defenses. China's reasoning is manipulative, for it uses North Korea's archaic Stalinist regime for diplomatic leverage; stalling, pleading, positioning Beijing as both compliant supplicant and moderate negotiator to false American belligerence. The game will only end when Seoul makes the call to implement integrated defense, breaking Beijing's patronage of Pyongyang.

If THAAD isn't willingly built, thwarting both Beijing and Pyongyang, then the sole remaining option is regime change. To acquire this objective, the US must prepare regional coalition members throughout Pacific East Asia to assist in diplomatic initiatives fostering stronger defenses, cutting down illicit trace and access to foreign goods that North Korea is desperate to have. Accomplishing this feat prepares the US to confront Beijing's international ambitions while addressing North Korean belligerence. Chess instead of checkers.

Housing Policies

The 2008 banking crisis originated with congressional mandates lowering underwriting standards to assist in the maintenance of social policies. It continues to this day, even after the crisis that nearly collapsed the entire US financial system and two terms of executive liberal governance. If anyone wants to discern why so many citizens remain angry and defiant at professional political classes, they have to examine US housing policy after the fall.

Both Fannie Mae and Freddie Mac are considered GSEs (government sponsored enterprises). They still embody profound residual risks to the union, and only an examination of the political agenda of both political parties can expose how GSEs rightfully contain future crises that must be resolved if US banking, credit, and equity markets are to regain stability. Some details are needed here. Fannie and Freddie engage in opaque and risky credit-risk transfers. Until these credit transfers are fixed, the entire continent is exposed to collapse.

To reduce having American working citizens pay to mop up future crises leveraged to high volatility, exposing US capital markets to systemic failure, these GSEs must transfer their credit risk portfolios before they acquire new loans. As of this writing, contemporary credit risk transfers are deliberately opaque debt instruments that historically imply explicit government guarantee. It must end. How to accomplish this goal without harming citizens who want the American dream? To begin, a synoptic approach to fiscal and monetary policy at the executive level must be addressed, maintaining the separation of powers doctrine. You see, Reagan's policy mix entailed politicizing the maintenance of legislation. In a word, politics. What Reagan accomplished with Volcker in advancing the United States out of fixed exchange rates toward a float while administering massive increases in GDP with monetarism must be applied to housing. Politics matters. Today's GSEs set the price of credit risk transfers based on calculations in politically allocated credit markets. Instead, they should engage in public transfer of said risks with private market participants, actively increasing the transparency of signals for everyone to witness. This means entire fiefdoms would be engaged in the maintenance of a market, like mortgage originators, mortgage insurers, and numerous other private entities. They would take the credit risk transfer before the loan is sold to Fannie or Freddie. Why isn't this a policy now? It's the identical reason why banks remain fragile by design. Washington's dominant political classes enjoy rent seeking and cheerleading, creating and sustaining self-perpetuating grievances for political exploitation. Insisting on any open rationale to alleviate this problem openly hurts professional politicians.

The Federal Housing Financing Authority has recommended that Fannie and Freddie develop and field transfers as open market participants. It will never happen because Congress passed the Federal Housing Finance Authorities Common Securitization Platform (CSP). This is nothing less than an official federal policy to insulate the GSEs from transparency. This new initiative will create and enforce GSEs to use an unassailable barrier to securitize debt outside the market. The effect is the nullification of price signals to evaluate the pricing, volume, and risk of securitized instruments. This is typical of any dominant political class. Don't reform anything, just build another bureaucracy. The absence of any future transparency in housing securitization created the very vortex that nearly brought down America.

The toxic twins are at it again.

The Bitch and Brawl: What Thatcher Teaches

The gift that modernity bequeathed was the discovery of consciousness and interiority. They never existed before in any regime ever until the American founding exploited or built on the social, political impact of revelation. Consciousness embodies the achievement that became interiority—the knowledge of distinctiveness as a universal. This achievement had its origin as a sacramental reality (e pluribus enum). A Greek insight could not find cultural affinity in Semitic thought given its propensity for static, positivist juridical thinking. This is significant because militant secularism is built on a Christian foundation of individual liberty. Individualism remains the altar upon which progressive thought seeks to expand the ever-widening gulf between ethics and progress. Thatcher saw it differently. So should the tenured radicals in history departments.

In 1975, Margaret Thatcher was the leader of Britain's opposition. She had her first meeting with a former governor of California named Ronald Reagan. The meeting was plain, uneventful, and embodied nothing special. An unpopular view shared between them was that the West was losing. Contrariness shaped both of them. Adversity proved worthy of both opponents, for soon thereafter, Reagan would need Thatcher's unyielding openness as she piled on, moving Reagan out from his liberal views of nuclear nonproliferation with Russia. Her openness and his temperament blended an unwritten agenda that would have defeated Reagan's tenure if made public. Let me explain.

Historians write history as if the arc of history is linear. It is never that way. The confrontation between Reagan and Gorbachev should be characterized as friendly. The hectoring Thatcher gave the Soviet leader was natural. She read him right, for he was seeing her as Reagan's best proxy. A difficult, nearly dreadful relation between her and Gorbachev was achieved. It was never written to be policy. It just happened. The tension between Thatcher and Gorbachev in London on their first meeting in 1984 was confrontational and wrought with disaster. She meant to lecture him on Western superiority; he dutifully took it in stride. Thatcher's anger at Reagan's SDI was real and enduring. She upbraided him continuously even in private and over the phone. Why? Because she thought his unrealistic dream of eliminating nuclear weapons at Reykjavik opened her political flank to dangerous levels of appeasement that she sought to desperately avoid at all costs. Her ardent belief in maintaining a favorable balance of power by fielding Trident submarines from England's North Sea was upset by Reagan's unilateral disarmament. She couldn't bear a nuclear-free Europe, nor could she bear having Russia drive wedges between the Atlantic Alliance, as Irish hunger strikers and South African apartheid did. In her thinking, the American president must be hectored into shelving utopian fantasies.

The trick in evaluating this epoch is to appreciate that life is lived simultaneously, not linearly. Because Thatcher possessed trustworthy independence consistently fortifying her openness, she could strike out in favor of pulling the president over to her political sentiments. Her fierce openness paid off because members of Reagan's staff were able to envelop her trail of enticements before policies or political sentiments overwhelmed them. Thatcher's independence taught Powell, Weinberger, and Shultz to trust their instincts. With the death of Chernenko, ideological affinities between executive staff in Downing and Washington began to grow in trends that simply would not have been overtly possible as policy. The overt Cartesian quality to the historian's craft damages the felt experience both leaders had upon embarking on their respective endeavors.

Even still, the women triumphed.

The Island Middle Kingdom, Reform, and Western Norms

Nien Cheng was a formidable woman. Having served in Mao's wedding party, she knew intimate details of his life that few understood, like his ability to absorb and project enormous tactical skill in dealing with superior mechanized foes; his resources for enduring severe deprivations served him well in China's civil war. He was a student of China's most difficult ethical and political quandaries. His Confucian reserve was tightly hewed from his knowledge of Sinic jurisprudence. This remained inseparable from the warring states period. Mao viewed himself and his leadership tactics outside Judeo-Christian norms. He remains sui generis. His romantic revolutionary appeal of the superiority of agrarian life was manufactured. A true totalitarian, everything was subjugated to serve the party. Everything. He ruled with no true rivals, and the consequences of his leadership were minimally acknowledged with age. True to form, he ignored the social, political, and spiritual catastrophe his policies had on China's political trajectory.

Mao's Cultural Revolution and Great Leap Forward directly contributed to the exhaustion of China and its consequent embrace of capitalism. Why, then, pursue it? The answer is discerned only when one acknowledges why Marxism was embraced.

Militant collectivist thought in Marxism had strong cultural affinities with Confucianism. But that's not the whole story, for the arrival of Imperial European civilization came an irritant that Chinese authorities were most reluctant to acknowledge—namely, the indigenous geopolitical and social ideals of the Middle Kingdom could not displace the achievement of a superior foe. Only with Marxism could China compete. But that struggle was dependent on having an easily ameliorated human person. That meant destroying the natural bonds of solidarity between family members, between lovers and friends. It meant that the personal became political. No sphere of autonomy was permitted. Mao reveled in supremacy; it brought China to the edge of collapse. Yet the cost for utopia was irrelevant. Like Germany under the twin yoke of social Darwinism and Jewish Bolshevism, it must be paid. And paid it was.

Having been released from long solitary confinement, Nien began a discreet investigation into her daughter's murder at the hands of Maoists. Having been CEO of British Petroleum Shell in Shanghai immediately made her and family members criminals. Her politically criminalized identity made her easy prey for rivals seeking advancement (remember, we always work toward the Fuhrer). The truth emerged slowly after her release from confinement. Having been rehabilitated, some spoke with caution and extreme reserve in telling of how her daughter was murdered. Not knowing how her daughter Meiping lived while imprisoned affected her health, her sanity. Now she knew. Meiping refused to slander her mother. Officials wrote of suicide. Nien knew better and moved to Washington, DC, to tell of a life lived in utopia.

Totalitarianism needs acquiescence. It lives on the lie. It cannot suffer the presence of rivals or sources of thought unconfirmed to its suffocating agenda. It first solicits then promises. The only refuge is conscience, and that, too, is weakened from natural, psychological, physical deprivation. Remember the satanic Teutonic retort, "Vee have r vays."

Like Germania, the ideals fortifying the widening gyre of totalitarian life are inseparable from geography, albeit without a neat determinism. For China, ideals of authority, the mandate of heaven, continuously originate from the north in Peking, in a concentric circle moving littoral south into its southern breadbasket, ending deep in the interior. Why? Because political legitimacy in China resonated from difficult northern highlands adjacent to its major interior rivers, for China's vision of itself was always fraught inward. Even today, Beijing's dominant threat remains its interior. Beijing spends more on internal security measures than all its defense spending. We should remember that as we seek to get Beijing's attention with its client state in Pyongyang or in flanking China's blue water strategy for Pacific dominance beginning in the South China Sea. We have options. China is best viewed as an island cut off from reliable neighbors. Just ask the Vietnamese. China, having witnessed massive migrations of young men from its interior toward urban Eastern littoral regions only to move again southward toward favorable manufacturing, has exhausted itself. For the second time in forty years, China is exhausted. This time, under an indigenous Western yoke of manufacturing. The tide now is reform. Contemporaries throughout the West speak of China moving toward a consumption-based political economy. It remains to be seen if Beijing can liberalize its current and capital account because a political economy based on tax revenue from domestic consumption isn't alloyed to the social, political ideals of enforced Confucian thought. Beijing, being unable to command the social, domestic heights of its own economy, would need to relinquish control. Given its geography and regional history, that's a good bet. But given the current state of digital technology, it remains to be seen if Beijing would accept such Western reform because it would mean the end of opaque politics emanating from Beijing. Having clear lines of authority similar to Western civil-military relations is not something Beijing aspires to. This is witnessed in the panic that has engulfed Chinese officials blamed for investment losses. Having forced government purchases to buy and hold market positions, there is no indigenous market to signal how to move positions into viable civilian-run autonomous markets. This fissure between government and everyone else cannot be unwound favorable to rebalancing without permitting the emergence of civil society. This gulf cannot be bridged favorable to the politics that has dominated Beijing for decades.

Having events dominate the professional technocrats has been very embarrassing to Beijing, which continues to pride itself on having mastered Western ways. Competitive devaluation and consequent importing of inflation aren't the stories. The real news is the awkward policy coordination that has permitted events to overwhelm Beijing. This isn't something the Chinese are used to, for it reveals just how far behind Beijing is in dealing with a market. Since competitive devaluation, the Chinese central bank reassured everyone to expect a policy regime tied to exchange rate stability. That never arrived. The yuan continued to fall anyway. Officials in Beijing began speaking of fiscal and monetary stimulus to maintain GDP growth target of 7 percent. This proved wrong too. Immediately after this pronouncement, General Secretary Xi emphatically stated that no such intervention was possible. Real interest rates (nominal plus inflation) throughout China have risen dramatically. Capital flight continues, and the Chinese are replacing lost liquidity as newly created reserves. The central bank in China is losing massive reserves that it stockpiled. All this continues to roll out while the dollar strengthens. This is how credit-driven booms end, with debt-to-GDP ratios approaching nearly 250 percent. How does this end?

Less intervention, stronger emerging civil society unhinged from the commanding opacity of Beijing would unleash the very faith needed to build structural reform and sustainable growth. Real market-orientated policy growth permits failure. It also allows for regeneration and growth of new industries. The American failure was similar in that our political class valued having the central bank prioritize market stability over independent price setting, creating massive distortions in bonds, asset bubbles, and exchange rates. For true reform to happen, the average citizen throughout China needs confidence that the state has interests beyond its own immediate ideological needs.

An insight Nien knew better than most. Rest in peace, dear friend, for they never broke you.

Solzhenitsyn: The Renewal

Alexander Solzhenitsyn's Harvard lecture remains astonishing in its prophetic insight regarding the weakness of libertine philosophies in America. He clearly could not have anticipated the Reagan Revolution. A conservative revisionist reading of that lecture is currently required in light of his study of Tocqueville and Reagan's renewed grasp of America exceptionalism. I am not advocating Solzhenitsyn's ignorance of our founding, just Reagan's advance. I am indicating that, absent his grasp of Reagan's political tradition, it remained outside Solzhenitsyn's prophetic admonishment of the West in his lecture. There remain reasons why. I hope to explain them here.

The American founding, particularly the Declaration and Constitution, were engendered both to preside over the governing architecture and to preserve the moral pluralism, grounding the revolution and establishing our experiment in democracy as a Constitutional Republic. All were slowly eroded by the birth of the Cold War and its fruits—namely, the welfare state.

Those who decried the end of the experiment in liberty need to recognize how domestic social and political events derailed the experiment. Civil War, Reconstruction, two World Wars, and the civil rights movement were required to perfect our commitment to democracy as liberty in equality. Even through this tumultuous phase in our history, the architecture was structured to the vision of the founders.

The Cold War and the welfare state displaced the relation between the individual, the state, and federalism. It actually displaced Jefferson's vision of how this great republic is to remain great through vibrant, small, committed personal hierarchies acting to preserve the moral mores in which liberty thrives. This displacement engendered the current tired ennui prevailing in our elite cultural institutions. Consequently it created a new humanism analogous to all failed utopian revolutions. It eliminated fragile spheres of interest and autonomy needed for the Jeffersonian vision. Instead we have a flaccid, therapeutic ethos that Alex Tocqueville so carefully demonstrated that democracies are capable of if equality becomes unhinged from the moral framework of Christianity. The 1970s displayed the altered soul of the American citizenry that was for Reagan to vanquish.

John Paul II carefully picked up on Tocqueville's premise in "Fides et Ratio (Faith and Reason)" in pursuing the dominate relations of nihilism, radicalized libertarianism, egalitarianism; all informed from abstractions about unhistorical ideals of the meaning of humanness. What Tocqueville and John Paul demonstrated is that political ideals and their conquering institutions, divorced from a true humanism, become so effete, so attenuated, it prevents self-defense.

Solzhenitsyn's lecture at Harvard reveals ignorance about an original hearing informed from both the Declaration and Constitution from which our representative republic emerged and sought renewal.

Still, how can renewal begin if the prophet never permits the probative value of his condemnation?

Solzhenitsyn simply could not imagine an unrealized future wherein a capitalist driven mercantile citizenry sought renewal by rededicating itself to an original heritage in our founding documents that the American left and the welfare state interrupted in favor of a Marxist socialist agenda.

When we immerse ourselves in the meaning of the founder's vision, we will free ourselves from an inherited tyranny born in revolutionary idealisms engendered unabated in a depersonalized culture so effectively depicted by both Orwell and Huxley. Both men knew and understood how the dream sought, fought, and toiled for by Hamilton, Madison, Washington, Adams, and Jefferson comes to us in earthen vessels, embodied principles neither self-executing nor self-sustaining.

The Cold War Child

Raymond Aron, Isaiah Berlin, Winston Churchill, and Pope John Paul II had much in common. Aron and the French left were ardent in their support of secular humanism that had its birth in 1789. Berlin was a deracinated Jew who firmly purchased a new life bequeathed to him by the British, most especially at Oxford, where he engagingly wrote on political issues that dominated the life of a don ensconced from the tragedy that befell those in Eastern Europe. Churchill understood and lived the perils that secular promise hailed. Although he did not drive deep into the theological foundation of freedom and liberty, he understood the relation. It fell to John Paul II to craft a final response to the question that dominated the life of Aron, Berlin, and Churchill.

Aron, Berlin, and Churchill were vexed to explore a moral dilemma around political lines of thought. All three men felt as Huxley or Orwell did, that modern man was incapable of managing a future. It fell to John Paul to quarry an answer opposing such a view. He lovingly answered in the affirmative that man was capable of a future, and he spent his time as bishop and pope deeply engaging the sources that renew civilization. Perhaps only two political writers came close to the thought of John Paul, it was Eric Voegelin and Arnold Toynbee, but neither had the position to both publicly embody and fortify the theological ground that informed freedom and liberty. John Paul II had both in spades.

Mid-twentieth century fiction writers like Aldous Huxley and Eric Blair (pen name: George Orwell) penned accounts of dystopic life under the rule of both consumerist and politically fascist tyranny. Both engaged the issues of their time as did Eric Fromm when he wrote Escape from Freedom, which portrays the types of personalities that desire domination. Fromm wrote that some men are not fit for liberty, so they wish to be dominated.

Can we discover the field that makes such men write as they do? Can we possess the vision they saw? Is it possible to know the question that dominated the lives of such men?

What these men bear witness to had profound political and social consequences. What they all witnessed was how human individuality became submerged by the giant scale upon which modern life was organized.

Only John Paul II had the intellectual fortitude to summon the resources of the church to defeat a moral question posed by the enlightenment. For the persons and institutions that originally framed such an insight had failed in providing a framework to modify or engage such an issue. One could argue that the American founding was the only political solution bearing such religious, moral sentiments. But now it flails as the West struggles to embrace new freedoms created from the light of such a forward-moving positivism.

If one were to study the political course upon which John Paul II tacked as he engaged a failed modernity, he unwittingly began by inserting his authority by consolidating the church. He performed such acumen with deftness. He understood that before he engaged others, his own house must be in order.

Nevertheless, it fell to the church to work out a theology of resistance to mass standardization, production, and consumption. For John Paul II and the abovenamed artists were affronted by how the human person became an appendage to consumption.

Winston Churchill has written about his hatred for the collectivization of life and thought that emanates modernity. In this, John Paul II was anticipated. Churchill wrote that he never believed that history was made by forces. He never denied that ideas had a powerful impact on the life of man. What Churchill denied was that ideas bear responsibility for shaping the future of man. For him, a world made by tides, tendencies, and not wisdom and virtue was worthy of repudiation. What both Churchill and John Paul II agree upon is this: Individual virtue can puncture the scale upon which man shapes his freedom.

If one studies the diaries of Churchill, you can anticipate a dominant theme: All around him were men drowning in crisis of abdication. From the World War I throughout World War II, the men who dominated the political scene were caught up in a world in which the character of men no longer was the dominate factor determining political trajectories. Instead of character, ideology became the axis upon which the future was determined. In this vein, all the writers mentioned above found much to repudiate. None other than John Paul felt compelled to author a response shaping an impact as bulwark against ideology in affirmation of human liberty. He began by discerning the interior contours of human sexuality. For John Paul, the sanctity of conjugal relations was the gift Revelation gave the West.

At the center of this ideological vortex was an error that needed remedy. John Paul II began his pontificate with the cry, "Do not be afraid." His battle cry to the ramparts of human freedom was a call to acknowledge that progress in the modern world was founded upon a false understanding of humanness. Ethics and progress need not be mutually exclusive in their engagement to procure the goods of this world. John Paul saw a profound error reminiscent of Churchill in that fortune was in constant hostility to virtue. For modern man to reclaim his freedom and love of liberty, the call to virtuous life required fortification. Why?

Because if human agency was swallowed up by the mass effects of contemporary life so that courage and genius appear impotent and irrelevant, John Paul was prepared to look foolish for the sake of the gospel.

His titanic effort to engage and vanquish the claims of modernity in his "Theology of the Body" is often misconstrued. That's because he was framing his thought from a classical insight of Aristotelian physics, long since lost and dismissed by the West—namely, the indissoluble truth grounding desire in biology. It is nothing less than a broadside to the masters of suspicion and their preeminence in Hegel and Kant.

Too often, contemporary theologians write and speak of the nature of the conjugal act as the centerpiece of his moral endeavor of renewal. Many forget how the quotidian and the poetic shaped his life, most especially regarding solitude and work. His "Theology of the Body" embraces a profound truth that most in the West willingly ignore—namely, how excessive leisure destroys and removes the stress required to shape effective responses. John Paul II, in writing his "Theology of the Body," was also taking aim at the Marxian view of manual labor and alienation, for only a poet could write of the healing effects of manual labor.

Both John Paul II and Churchill wrote lovingly of the effects of manual labor, especially regarding the need that ethics inform our understanding of the relation between labor and capital or shape utopian ideologies that wreak havoc upon the political relations of men.

These insights were never acclaimed by Platonists like the Ayatollah Khomeini. Although neither man wrote explicitly against social Darwinism, Freud, or behaviorism, one cannot deny that such ideologies required a response.

What made John Paul II great?

His attachment to defending the religious ground of freedom and liberty. His unshakeable belief that the very constitution of man is religious.

And why would he succeed?

Because in defending such ideals and such truth, he was, as always, being true to himself.

Irving Kristol, Isaiah Berlin, Norman Podhoretz: Marxian Shylock's and the Political Incubus of Failure

The cherished yet divided life of diasporic Jews in America exemplified in Kissinger, Abraham Joshua Heschel, Irving Kristol, Isaiah Berlin, Norman Podhoretz, Einstein, and hosts of other brilliant minds relieved from the tyranny of Fascism in Europe was on full display last September in memory of Irving Kristol's death; as Americans favorably considered the Jewish embrace of liberalism, the

Democratic Party post–World War II and its intellectual achievements from Roosevelt down to Johnson's domestic resolve reveal an intellectual reversal fit for Sophocles.

Who else to quarry the threads leading to a birth of a new order demonstrated in Reagan? A birth, whose pangs ran deep within the life of Irving Kristol himself. As we travail the reversal, the contours of those mentioned above, we arrive at a deadly earnest for whom only the most ardent and sincere would survive. For if Whittaker Chambers's passionate reluctance ran foul, who else would survive the turning back? Among those privileged either to know Irving Kristol himself or the ideals that beckoned him, one thing was clear, the man had the courage of his convictions.

Irving Kristol, Isaiah Berlin, and many other intellectual Jews of the wartime period exemplified a seriousness of mind that is permanently amiss from the clerics of our time. It's difficult to exhort to another the power that ideas held over many between 1880 and 1947. American innocence did not suffer as did France in the First World War. We embodied that innocence to a fault. Yet it, too, paid interest under Marshall. How to reveal the passionate innocence open to being shaped by a cold, calculating foreign rubric that became Marxism? Kristol, Berlin, Podhoretz, and legions gave themselves over to a lie that hardened them to a political and intellectual reversal that blazes America today.

How did it begin?

The life of a diasporic Jew can ask what others can't witness. Can the Torah shape an answer to the challenges of secularism and the appeal to modernity? Is such an answer appealing? Can a love of Israel embodied as an eternal promise be enough? Is not the response of witnessed exile the full embodiment of a felt integrity par excellence? And what of the ovens?

In the end, many such Jewish intellectuals knew that sentiments alone were insufficient. To survive, Israel and its heritage must allow itself to partner outside its tradition. The geopolitical challenges threatening it were insurmountable. It either maintained a rigid posture of unaccommodation or vanish in another onslaught. Kristol,

Berlin, and Podhoretz tried and succeeded in finding the needed resolution in neoconservatism.

In lieu of Kristol's death, conservatives and Marxists witnessed a metanoia unbecoming political life. For the Jew who remembers the heady nights of fin de siècle Paris, New York, or London, the West was expected to fail in light of the fierce convictions of those passionately wedded to determinism. There are lessons here for those who believe that passion alone is sufficient to effect political desire. We should quarry Kristol's decisive turn away from Marxism to find a Socratic mien known as intellectual responsibility.

Only those who openly acknowledge the burden of liberty, the fragility of the means required to live in accord with conscience, and the terrible challenges that secularism brings to both American Jewry and exceptionalism can understand the price paid from turning away from the cherished beliefs of one's youth.

Irving Kristol's reversal, achievement, and consequent anniversary is monumental when you consider the sheer force of his personal challenge: the belief that ideas matter.

There is within such people an optimism born from and informed by the tempered solitude of textuality; a Strauss, Tocqueville, or Burke.

Being a head of his time, we see him in Leon Kass's admonishment that contemporary life, being indebted to a Jewish diaspora, shaped its contact from Anglo liberty openly. A constant tension between Athens and Jerusalem only resolved in favor of Rome or Washington. In a word, reason.

We can submit that very few people ever see the shape of their convictions embodied in the drive of citizenry, in framed institutions worthy of sacrifice or commitment. As such, Kristol and the others are the worthy stepchildren of our founders. For them, Zionism emptied herself from ghettos of Europe to embrace the prophetic ethos of modernity outside the moral and liturgical traditions of their faith. For them alone, Revelation was not abandoned, it was a politically acceptable alternative given the time and choice. If America, and by extension the free world, was to win in the battle between liberty (America) and equality (Russia), then nationhood as understood within the confining traps of geopolitical strategy must be renewed from within.

They began the step to thwart an impending demise by choosing liberty over determinism. The personal price paid was steep. Longtime friends and lovers fiercely attacked them as traitors. All wrote personal accounts of the social and psychological impact of such encounters. Remember Chambers and the epiphany of his recognized daughter. The strained witness of relief only to surrender to the mystery that is a grace communicated to the soul alone. In such, he held company with Thomas More, Dostoyevsky, and Solzhenitsyn. Not bad company. But the price was steep, nonetheless. As such, he put faith in integrity over social status or the false conviction of consistency that fortifies useful idiots. Because he pressed onward alone, like Lincoln, we have a future today.

The birth of neoconservatism is witnessed in the mature reversal of several men and women committed to the belief that man is free, and everywhere, he is in chains.

Why Debt Ceilings Matter: Governance

In national emergencies, Congress can exceed tax expenditures and run deficits. What Reagan taught was simple. The deficit itself is not the problem; but the depth, the reach, and scope of government on civil society is a serious problem.

This is why confiscatory taxation or, more importantly, the philosophy animating the convictions of progressives is so dangerous. For progressives, there is no limiting principal. Taxes will never catch up to the spendthrift mores of any political class. This is why conservatives often use moral terminology when criticizing excessive annual spending; we lose more of our sovereignty each time. Just ask state governors.

This is why raising the debt ceiling is such a bad idea. Raising the debt limit allows congressional members a way out from having to accept responsibility for large public expenditures. We've surpassed $17 trillion this year alone. And that does not even mention the social mandates that are around $50 trillion. Do the math. We don't have an economy that large.

Debt ceilings provide a false sense of security. But this sentiment never acknowledges the reason why we surpass the ceiling every year. We run chronic deficits because our economy isn't growing.

The Federal Reserve has helped in keeping interest rates low. The interest paid to US Treasury holders (US bondholders) determines that requisite revenue needed to service such debt. By keeping the rate low, the Central Bank is helping a spendthrift Congress continue financing mandates or expenditures that are clearly broken. If the interest rate should rise, more debt instruments must be issued.

The debt burden on the economy is measured in relation to GDP. The CBO now states that our current account of issued debt is 70 percent of annual GDP. Before the 2007 recession, it was 39 percent.

Okay, so what's the problem?

A growing and unsustainable debt level manifests an expansion of government. Philosophically this means that government must confiscate more sovereignty from civil society to fuel its expansion. The debt ceiling has not been an effective instrument in controlling debt. It has led to a dreadful complacency.

Most states require a balanced budget; yet the growth of federal mandates to the exclusion of federalism only exacerbates state budgets. All that's left are budgetary gimmicks.

A real debt-ceiling limit would control spending directly. A rule would be to bring government outlays into historic ratios relative to GDP.

Let's start there.

The State Pension Blowout

When Meredith Whitney, the chief investment officer for Kenbelle Capital CP, published Fate of the States: The New Geography of American Prosperity, most folks never really questioned the contractual obligations states have; the mantra out of union leadership was that such obligations were safe from bankruptcy.

Imagine that.

Well, it turns out that the vast majority of states throughout our union haven't funded pension obligations. That's called bankruptcy. And the same union officials continue to shield this nasty reality behind rhetoric that really is propaganda. Because states have the constitutional and legal authority to tax, they cannot file bankruptcy. So as union officials continue to mask paper-thin obligations behind opaque rhetoric, let's keep in mind that bankruptcy proceedings are about restructuring the very obligations unions erroneously think are safe.

Thanks to QE, public pension benefits are really well capitalized. Asset classes remain well capitalized. However, public pension costs have soared.

Let's look at three land mines. California, Detroit, and Chicago.

Chicago must make $1 billion pension contribution this year alone, a third of the cities operating budget. Just this year alone. Their pension debt is $19.4 billion. Chicago just released a massive amount of unsecured debt. It issued $500 million in commercial paper and $900 million in general obligations. Can you believe that?

Detroit is worse. The city is expecting to go broke by 2020. As a city, Detroit is expecting to repay its general obligation bondholders $0.20 on the dollar while suing to invalidate $1.4 billion in certificates of participation that were used to backfill 2005 pension costs. Try not to laugh. The banks that fostered this merely asked Detroit to perform an interest rate swap. These banks will now only be paid 30 percent of their investments. Oh yeah, unions refuse to support a readjustment plan to repay the banks in total.

Throughout the city, Detroit is cutting pension benefits 34 percent. Although these retirees can recoup their losses if the market performs well.

California: The City of Stockton filed for bankruptcy in 2012. The Franklin Templeton Investments is only recovering $94,000 from its initial $35 million investment. Its investors will receive about fifty cents on the dollar. See where this is going; bankruptcies remain the venue of choice for debt obligations but pensions remain untouched. Why is this a problem? Cities throughout California continue to muddle through each year with most having to restructure annually. Refusal to face the political third rail of pensions isn't a sound fiscal strategy going forward anymore.

Unions throughout this nation continue to placate everyone or anyone to the mantra that pension obligations are protected by state and federal constitutions protecting them from impairment.

Come again?

The BS of Secular Stagnation

Secular stagnation is deliberate obfuscation. It locates any difficulty within the business cycle itself, absolving the very policy makers from having to admit failure. It didn't work for the Mayans throughout Central America; it will not work for progressives.

Being reluctant to admit policy failure is tantamount to death. Neither Islamists nor Western progressives can admit to spheres of authority outside approved master narratives. Sad, isn't it? We thought the adults ran the show. They don't.

By any measure, median incomes have fallen in America. This is because the medium of exchange itself is destroyed. Nevertheless, high wage earners haven't suffered under this monetary or executive regime. As Washington centralizes more grasp over civil society, it reaches the point of diminished returns. We're there now. Power or influence in civil society is completely decentralized. Not in Washington. As the increase in reach and scope of government continues to devour the very capital needed to sustain any enduring achievement, more spheres of American life are tuning out and going native or rogue. This isn't good. The commanding heights of once formal social or political institutions that served the means of assimilation are no more. The blight is real, and it isn't coming back.

As the concentration of wealth and opportunity begins to shrink, we should anticipate an exacerbated comity characterizing defeat.

Remember the age of Reagan, rising living standards, massive social mobility, real wage growth, disinflation, opening of markets, and new technology. His economy grew on average 7 percent in real terms. GDP was a persistent 4.6 percent with sound dollar appreciation. Marginal tax rates were combined at 28 percent.

It all started during the second quarter of 1983.

What can the GOP do? It can begin making the case between collectivism and income inequality. The means used are fiscal, monetary, and philosophical. In a word: leadership.

Where else do we see the embodied mess that is collectivism?

While citizens are denied the ability to get to equity or capital formation, fat-boy government programs run amuck with bloated phony expansions of politically allocated credit. All at the continued expense of savers and those who struggle with new businesses or new business models.

Oh, and that unemployment rate? Well, the growth of government underwrites phony job numbers. Yes, it's that bad.

So if the GOP is serious, it will use the debt limit as a national referendum on the size, scope, and shape of government with real legislative budgetary controls that limit spending, not just a reduction in the rate of spending growth.

We need fiscal reform from the House, reform for how the House conducts legislative business, the restoration of income growth, and tax reform. How about a real slowdown in automatic entitlement growth, serious pay cuts for congressional members or staff, and elimination of subsidized benefits until resolution.

Let's face it; fat-boy government drives inequality.

Sex and the City

I remain dismayed when people use any kind of moral equivalency. An example is the wall of apartheid (originally coined by Jimmy Carter) concerning the West Bank in Israel. Anyone with even a modicum of knowledge of the politics throughout the Near East knows why the Israelis built the wall. It was not for the purpose of preventing suicide bombers. It was to anticipate a very ugly political and cultural reality, one seen in Northern Ireland, the United States, any wealthy cities throughout South America and most certainly South Africa. I'm talking about persistent low fertility rates.

The Israelis are trying to keep Israel Jewish by keeping a firm hold on voting districts in light of skyrocketing fertility rates among Arab women throughout the West Bank.

The pill and other social, monetary, and ideological means have weakened the West. Western Europe has been on a demographic decline for decades. With the arrival of illegal immigrants throughout the United States, our fertility rates are actually up. But persistently low fertility throughout first world nations is already dangerously low. We are only witnessing the initial social impact of such demographic trends.

In order for a country to maintain a steady population, it needs a fertility rate of 2.10; since the 1960s, fertility rates in first world nations have plummeted. The hysteria of any Malthusian apocalyptic vision was always false. Norman Bourlag defeated Malthus. Period.

Historically population contraction has never been accompanied by prosperity. The West only has chronicled two experiences analogous to our declining fertility: The Black Death of Europe and the Fall of Rome.

Low fertility is also the dirty little secret for why or how American entitlement expenditures are broken. As the population shrinks, we will experience the following: a quickly shrinking tax base due to labor force contraction, and skyrocketing costs for pensioners and those on permanent heath care, etc. As demand sputters downward, price discovery and monetary stability violently contract.

How else to say it: low fertility is modernity's great trap.

The Social Crisis of the American Working Class

Charles Murray of the American Enterprise Institute in Washington remains the single most significant sociologist since the passing of Seymour Martin Lipset. His latest is titled The State of White America. This is a startling account of reversal of America's once robust civic culture. Murray has warnings similar to John Paul II.

America is unraveling.

America is coming apart at the seams, not the seams of race or ethnicity but of class.

For a nation that has committed itself to egalitarian principles, this seems wrong, except for the traditional relation between natural law and equality. Murray reveals that America has always had the emergence of class primarily informed from core behaviors and values. That core was Judeo-Christian. Sever that link and you erase the American dream.

Murray identifies specific founding virtues such as marriage, industriousness, and religious identity that has always been considered the social basis for self-government. This book reveals two worlds (upper middle or working class) increasingly separate and unequal.

Unwed mothers alone are 50 percent. In 1960, it was barely 5 percent.

The revolution in the separation of the classes can only be accounted in light of the total abandonment of Judeo-Christian morality.

Simply put: secularization is far more pronounced in the working class. Its impact will continue unabated especially considering the requirements for social mobility—namely, high-skilled labor, mobility, and industriousness required for social stability. The American working class is getting cut off from the richest sources of both self-renewal and social capital: marriage by two-parent families.

What's taking its place?

A working class characterized by men who cannot discipline themselves to become credentialed out of manual labor and minimum wage. Women who cannot accept the self-discipline to acknowledge the absolute necessity to keep the conjugal act within the framework of permanent commitment (marriage). In a sentence, we are quickly finding ourselves unsuited for the strict requirements of both self-government or citizenry in a free society.

Both Alex Tocqueville and Francis Ground were correct in relating the significance of mores to a sound republic. "The American Constitution is remarkable for its simplicity; but it can only suffice a people habitually correct in their actions." It's simple, change the domestic habits of the Americans, their love of religious devotion, their high respect for morality, and it will not be necessary to change a single letter of the Constitution in order to vary the whole form of government.

The war against the secular masters is already on its way.

How do we win?

We defend the indissolubility of marriage, the sanctity of the conjugal act, and the inviolability of the human person.

We defend life.

A Party Divided: Election 2018 in Connecticut

It was one week out before the convention, and here I was, sitting in a diner at eight o'clock on a Sunday morning in Waterbury, Connecticut, with my field director. We were there because we had scheduled a breakfast meeting with delegates to the State Convention from the area. On the drive there, I couldn't help but notice both the beauty and decay of the great state of Connecticut. Years of Democrat-controlled government at almost all levels had caused communities that were once known for housing great companies and on lists of some of the best places to live in America to now making it on lists for the highest rates of unemployment and the highest rates of drug overdoses. No areas seemed more forsaken and hit hardest than the blue-collar communities of our state, where many Democrats had failed to live up to their promises election cycle after election cycle. All this made it feel all that much more worthwhile for me to give up one of my mornings on a day when I usually go to church with my family and instead spend some time to hear the stories of the residents in these kinds of communities. Communities such as the valley towns and small rural areas like in Eastern Connecticut were often ignored by many of the other candidates rather choosing to campaign harder and more frequently in higher-delegate areas. For me, however, it was more about quality than it was quantity. I wanted that anyone who could spare the time to sit and have a conversation with me would leave knowing they had a friend in me and someone who cared about their town and their community more so than any other candidate. As I sat there having coffee with my field director, a group of friendly faces turned their heads toward me as they entered through the diner door. I remember the warm and excited looks on their faces. I also remember thinking to myself they can't surely be directing that smile and enthusiasm toward me. There must be someone sitting behind us that they recognize. However, as they came closer, it became clearer that they had come for our meeting as scheduled. My field director and I immediately rose from our seats to greet them. I remember their firm handshakes and genuine smiles. They had come from various delegations, and even though they didn't all end up voting for me during the convention, it was clear that Republicans were fired up this election cycle and were encouraged by the prospect of a true outsider conservative candidate. During this meeting, we discussed a wide range of issues facing the state, including taxes, tolls, the heroin and opioid crisis, the state budget, and state labor contracts. We also discussed how I planned to defeat the democratic opponent should I be the nominee of our party. I recall explaining to them that if I were to be the eventual nominee that we would need to organize a coalition like President Trump's when he won the presidential election in 2016. That we would need to create a coalition that included people who were disillusioned with the Democratic Party but who would not come out to vote for a Republican unless that Republican was willing to really stand for what he or she believed in and who wasn't looking to continue business as usual in Hartford. We needed someone who would not be afraid to call things out by their name and challenge the hereditary political power locked under the gold dome in Hartford. People in communities like Waterbury and the Northwest and Northeast corners needed to know what was going to be done to save their jobs from leaving the state because some employers might no longer be able to keep the lights. The climate seemed perfect for an outsider such as me to really shake things up and deliver a message that both the people and the politicians needed to hear. The group seemed impressed by my plans, but I think they were more impressed by the energy that we created. A woman said to me, "Mr. Lumaj, you sure are a breath of fresh air." Two hours had gone by just like that, and we all needed to be on our way.

In the following days, I would have many more meetings just like this one all over the state. With convention day approaching, we were booking meetings from as early as seven o'clock in the morning to late-night dinners. My whole team and I really wanted to perform well at the convention and win it outright if we could.

It was less than a year ago that we weren't sure if we were going to qualify financially for the state grant through what is known in Connecticut as the citizen's election program, which is a program that gives candidates running for statewide offices a certain amount of money for both the primary and the general election, if and only if they can raise a designated amount of money themselves. In my case for governor, that designated amount was $250,000 in increments of $100 or less. Quite the daunting task for nearly all candidates. During this time, we had to split our time between setting up fund-raising events and hitting the RTC trail. It was really a grueling period for all candidates. No matter how good of a fundraiser you think you may be, it is always a hard thing to do to ask someone for money no matter who you are. For me that was always a difficult task. I really did find it hard to be able to do that. During this time, we focused a lot on events in the Albanian American community throughout Connecticut. I knew that I needed them to get involved big time if I were to have a shot at raising this insane amount of money and in such small increments at that. Although this period was a struggle, it was also the time period when I was most inspired and motivated to run for governor of Connecticut. All the people who I would meet at these fundraisers really brought home the idea of who I was doing this for. It was for the hardworking, average, everyday American, who is working two or three jobs and barely making ends meet, but have not given up hope and are still fighting and getting involved and trying to support the right candidate. The pressure was great, but I knew that my heart and mind were both in the right place. On many occasions during these fundraisers, people would share with me their stories and sometimes their suggestions for when or if I got into office. I loved listening to people. I encountered people from all walks of life on this campaign and got to know the communities of towns from all over the state from Thompson to Greenwich and from Lakeville to Stonington. It was truly an amazing journey.

One of the he biggest fundraisers any candidate did that cycle in one night was the fundraiser I did in the Albanian American community in Waterbury. Nearly seven hundred people attended, most of them Democrats, willing to support an outsider, and we raised tens of thousands of dollars that night and had a great time doing it. It seemed at the time that we were a front-runner. As the fund-raising wrapped up, the political operations began to uptick. Going into the New Year, we had almost finished raising the money, and RTC visits became the number one priority. We split up our team. Each senior staff member would be assigned a different territory that they were in charge of. The primary objective was to make as many RTC visits as possible in towns and cities where we had a shot at picking up delegates. While at the same time revisiting towns where we had a stronghold in order to make sure we maintained that support leading up to the convention. The schedule was very tough for me. Working a full-time job and then having to travel all over the state was at times exhausting. I would normally get up at five o'clock and not be home until ten or eleven sometimes. I don't think any other candidate maintained a schedule that was this busy. I would never regret it though. After every single time I would do an RTC, I would walk out of that RTC invigorated and happy that I had the opportunity to speak to them.

Our journey, however, was not always this straightforward. There were many instances during the campaign trail where competitors and their campaigns really crossed the line, and I began to really question whether the Republican Party in Connecticut had ventured so far off the grid and willing to say and do anything to give their sides the upper hand that they were no longer the party or the people I knew. What I am about to share next is going to be a series of examples all true and not in the least bit exaggerated. All these examples can be verified by the eyewitnesses' accounts of those involved in this recollection I am about to share. Some of these identities I will not share and some I will. Some of these individuals in the stories I am about to share are current elected officials, others former party officials, and a slew of other individuals involved during the campaign process. Many of these people are household names in

Connecticut Republican politics and have built their political careers and reputations being known as people of high character and leaders in their communities. Claiming to protect the very same values that they themselves, as I am about to show you, betrayed. During this time, I would also like to mention those men and women who kept their promise and their word and helped the campaign tremendously. For as many episodes of betrayal and sleight, there were also great memories, moments that I shared with the many friends I made throughout this journey, friends that I still keep in touch with to this day. These were the people of great integrity and honor who stuck it out with me through the good and bad times. They truly believed in me and my campaign and stood with me through thick and thin.

The first of many that I would like to call out is none other than the establishment queen herself, House Minority Leader Themis Klarides. Themis is the second highest-ranking leader in our party, someone who, in the midst of a budget crisis, found herself in an advantageous position to pass a conservative budget through the house. A budget that even had the support of some house Democrats, but she squandered the opportunity and put the ball back in the Democrats' court. What eventually passed was a Democratic budget that was filled with more and more spending than the year before. In the midst of this whole situation in Hartford, she was also very politically active behind the scenes. No one can blame her or anyone for that matter for having an opinion on which candidate they would prefer, especially in her case, as she would be working directly with the new governor for the next four years. However, one thing that I have never taken too kindly to is threats, whether that is threat of physical harm or otherwise, and I especially don't take to kindly to threats made against my friends and those who supported my campaign. During the campaign trail, my team and I frequently visited the area that Themis represents. We campaigned very hard in the valley, an area where our message really resonated and where we found support among the people and the future delegates, with the exception of a few party elites who did not want the status quo to be interrupted by an outsider like me and who did not want someone who was not a part of their inner circle to take any piece of the political pie. House

Minority Leader Themis Klarides was one of these people. Upon discovery of an endorsement in the Naugatuck valley area from a delegate in one of the towns she represents, she became deeply troubled and angry with this individual for having the audacity to break rank and side with a non–Themis Klarides and establishment-approved candidate. She became so irate and felt her authority so threatened by what she perceived to be mutiny in her ranks that what she did next, according to a phone call received by one of my staffers by the said delegate, was astounding. This person was threatened to have their position within the party removed. They were also threatened to have their entire political future put in jeopardy if this person did not cooperate with Themis's commands, and there was also indication that maybe this person's livelihood could be put in jeopardy as well. This delegate was clearly very concerned by the threats that they had just received and asked to have the endorsement they gave retracted, fearing the possible ramifications that may ensue toward them if they did not cooperate. Others involved in intimidating and threatening this person were Shelton mayor Mark Lauretti and Seymour mayor Kurt Miller who went on to be our party's nominee for comptroller. This wouldn't be the first time Mark tried to pull a dirty trick on a member of his own party. Mark Lauretti betrayed the party and our nominee when he challenged Bob Stefanowski for the independent party line after already having endorsed him for governor, but I will get into that later down the road. For some reason, this particular delegate drew a lot of attention from many candidates and people involved with the party. Our campaign had also received information that Tim Herbst tried to talk them out of endorsing me and to endorse him. Tim was most likely the Themis Klarides–approved candidate for governor that I was referring to earlier. It would make sense seeing as how Tim would oftentimes reminisce on the campaign trail recounting the days when he used to intern for Themis at the legislature and now relished in the thought of serving alongside his mentor now that he was all grown up. I ultimately did decide to accept this delegate's retraction of their endorsement of me and agreed to pull it off my website in order to prevent any potential harm to him that could have come out of this. Now, I am aware of the fact that campaigns and even candidates have at times the need to use aggressive tactics. I myself have openly and aggressively criticized my competitors on various platforms when I didn't agree with what they were saying, either from a policy standpoint or when I felt they were saying or holding a position that was hypocritical when compared to their records in some cases. My staff was also relentless on the phones, bringing up the hypocrisy of some of these candidates who would vow to decrease taxes and who were supposedly social conservatives when their personal beliefs on social issues showed the opposite and their records as mayors and elected officials showed a record of increasing, not decreasing taxes. For example, the fact is that many of these candidates who were running for governor now had increased taxes and mill rates multiple times during their tenures in their towns and cities. My staff did a great job at highlighting these things, but we never engaged in threats or any other shameful and destructive tactics like some of our opponents and their allies. During the campaign, there were cases when some of our delegates would stray away and needed to be brought back in, but I never threatened them in any capacity in order to bring them back to our side, and no one on my team would have either or I would have immediately fired them. Regardless, many campaigns and outside influencers did engage in this kind of behavior as the house minority leader did and many others during the course of the campaign. Which brings me to my next example.

Jerry Labriola was a failed state party chairman who had to step down before he would have been brutally defeated in the election. Jerry always came off to me as a nice person, a little quirky and probably didn't know what he was doing the entire time he was party chairman for Connecticut but always came off as generally a nice guy. Little did I know that for weeks, behind the scenes leading up to the convention, Jerry Labriola had hopped on the Erin Stewart for Governor bandwagon. He thought he had picked a winner in this governor's race with choosing her. Something that even Stewart ultimately wasn't sure she wanted to do. Jerry, in his role as advisor or consultant for Stewart, thought that it would be a good idea, given the fact that he was a mastermind political operative, to try and slander me over the phone with my delegates. Jerry said things like "Peter doesn't look or sound American" very straightforward. He believed that I did not have the right to run for office because he believed only people who fit the traditional mold of what he believed was an American should be allowed to run for office. It is precisely the despicable people like Jerry who sometimes gives the Republican Party a bad name. What really angered me the most was not necessarily his comment per se but that he had the audacity to try this ploy so freely among delegates and think that they would be as twisted as he and that it would work and that he was well respected enough that word would not get out that it was he who was trying to spread this idea. Well, it didn't work, and shame on Erin Stewart who must have known Jerry was saying this. Erin claims to be an inclusive mayor of a big and diverse city—namely, New Britain. A city whether she realizes or not is filled with people who are immigrants like me. Jerry's insults got their just deserts. I happened to run into him at an event in Southeastern Connecticut where he was parading his candidate Erin Stewart around. I made a sarcastic remark about needing to be American to attend this event. I did it in a very light and joking manner but not directly letting him know what I knew. That my campaign staff had gotten information from one of our delegates about what Jerry had said about me a couple of weeks back. It quickly hit him like a ton of bricks as to what I was referring to. He almost immediately started sweating and became visibly shaky and nervous, his voice quivered, and he was stumbling on his words. He was trying to find room in the crowded lobby to make an escape. It looked as if he had a bad case of diarrhea and really needed to go. I was just standing there having a laugh. It was very entertaining to see. Meanwhile I had yet to really say much to him. I was simply standing there and mingling with others in the crowd as my field director Joe was doing the same. Jerry finally mustered the courage to utter something, having backpedaled for a few moments now. He was about twenty feet away when he said, "I'll catch you next time, Peter. Nice talking to you. Bye now." Jerry clearly knew at that point that based off my tone, I knew what he had done. Whether he was ashamed or frightened at my confrontation of him or both, I must say that the reaction was priceless, and I really enjoyed it. Ultimately the effect of his reckless remarks was not too terrible, and it did not work on my strong group of supporters.

Moving on, we have now none other than Tim Hebrst and the most entertaining saga in recent Connecticut Republican history. Tim and I had many skirmishes on the campaign trail. Let's first begin with the debates. The first debate that really defined our rivalry was the second GOP gubernatorial debate at RHAM High School in Hebron, Connecticut. During most of the first half of the debate, candidates, not including myself, were answering questions with scripted lines and canned answers. This was Mark Boughton's first debate, and he was dictating the tempo of the debate, talking about his record as mayor of Danbury. The flow of the debate was relatively smooth, quiet. I knew that I had to be the one to really shake things up and really take all these career politicians to task on their records. The most flagrant liar of them all was Tim Herbst. He claimed that he had lowered taxes in Trumbull many times, and that he had completely flipped the town of Trumbull around and that's why he was running for governor and not for another term for mayor. He also brought up some obscure measure for why he was the most deserving candidate to be governor because of his performance against Denise Napier four years ago, which, mind you, was still a loss. I couldn't take it anymore. This guy was standing there and manipulating and distorting the truth and thought that he was going to get away with it because he had stumbled upon a debate stage where no one was prepared to challenge him. However, I was. During the break between the two halves of the debate, I consulted with my team, and we really needed to hit him hard and where it hurt. We knew Tim would stand there all night and manipulate and distort the truth in his favor, so we had to hit hard and throw him off his game. One of my first statements in the second half was to call out each candidate by name and criticize them for their hypocrisy. I began by citing how each one of them had in one capacity or another voted or enacted measures to grow government. Mark Boughton, Dr. Prasad, Mark Lauretti, and Tim Herbst. They all raised their hands anxiously to respond to me, secretly probably loving what I did because it now gave them an opportunity to speak more. Which then, if they mentioned my name, I would have the green light to then strike back at them. The most bothered by my statements was Tim Herbst. Tim came back at me furiously, touting his tenure and that I didn't understand what it is like to hold office and get a call from your fire or police chief at three o'clock in the morning. I simply responded, "Well, I may have never held a job in the public sector, but Tim has never held one in the private sector," making it clear that he had been a career politician.

Tim reacted furiously. "Why are you lying?" he yelled. The truth is that I wasn't really too far off. If you did the math, there really isn't much there other than his years in office, in the legislature, or running for office. Tim was so visibly distraught during this debate that the press even described him as "a red-faced Tim Herbst."

It was here that the rivalry with Tim really began. We would go at it in other debates as well, but there was nothing like the second debate in Hebron. It garnered the most media attention for my campaign out of all the campaigns. The coverage was disproportionately portraying me in a negative light as only being an aggressor, but nonetheless, we had made the headlines, and there was at least some mention of the points I made during the debate. After that, I really became the favorite target of the media and the favorite target for Tim Herbst and his campaign. So much so that Tim began a separate campaign dedicated only to smear me. His point of attack was to tell delegates over the phone that I was not a real lawyer. The claims were that I had not received the right qualifications to practice law and that I was somehow able to fraud my way over the years as a fake attorney. He also accused me of harboring a convicted felon on my campaign. Another claim that was completely false. Tim continued to spread these rumors throughout the delegate pool, and my campaign inevitably got word of it. Tim had been using tactics similar to these all throughout the campaign ever since the beginning, when he was questioning why some of my donations like many of his had come from out of state, always trying to push a narrative that I was somehow a suspicious candidate. But this time, he was really stepping up the desperate attacks and trying to get personal. Tim always feared me. He feared having to compete with me on a primary ballot. He knew that primary voters would see that I was the true conservative and that he quite simply didn't have the conservative record to back him up. He also knew, as did many other of my competitors, that the best way to beat me was to unite forces and prevent me from reaching 15 percent at the convention, which would have allowed me ballot access during the Republican primary. And the best way to do this was to create these false stories and claims against me and get them out to as many delegates' ears as possible before and during the convention. Tim's campaign was the most negative out of all. My team quickly moved to dispel these blatant lies and made-up stories. Staying true to my policy of being transparent, we provided any proof that was necessary if delegates ever brought up the false rumors. As I mentioned, this rivalry between Tim and me would continue all the way up to the convention where backroom deals were done among several candidates for various offices to make sure that I didn't have the delegates to enter a primary. We'll discuss that more later.

The media is just as guilty of a culprit in the brining down of Republicans as any other force, if not more. In my case, leading up to the convention, the media seemed to have had made it their job to try and tear me and my campaign down. So much so that the CT Post had planned for a hit piece against me. They wanted to slander my name. They could not stand the idea of seeing me succeed. The corrupt liberal media like anywhere else is obsessed with destroying the reputations of conservative candidates. They hated me for the things that I stood for. They believed that someone who came to the United States as a refugee shouldn't be embracing conservative principles; that I needed to be a mouthpiece for the far-left liberals and the Democratic Party; that I, as a refugee, needed to be talking about how bad Trump is and how backward the Republicans are; that conservativism is not the way; and that socialism is what we need. While it is true, as I pointed out earlier and will continue to point out, that there are some bad actors within the party, that does not define who the whole party is and what we stand for as Republicans. Jerry Labriola does not stand for what the Republican Party stands for. That's why he was ousted. He is an outlier. The same goes for Tim

Herbst, as proven by the primary that only saw him get 17 percent of the vote. I will always be a Republican, and I will not shy away from supporting Donald Trump. I believe in him and his policies. They are what is needed for this country. I will never let myself become a pawn of the leftist, socialist, liberal media. As I said in a press conference, which I did immediately after this hit piece came out from the CT Post, "If I had been a liberal, I would have been your darling." That is 100 percent, without a doubt, true. The way that the liberal media treats those who are not of the same political persuasion is disgusting. They have no interest in protecting immigrants or refugees or anyone. They only seek power to enforce their socialist agenda of command and control. The liberal media had no interest in publishing my ideas on how to fix the state. They did not care to really have the conversations that needed to be had with regards to the disastrous condition of our state. How I had planned on renegotiating the state employee contracts with right-to-work legislation. Or how I was the only one talking about our decaying cities, running rampant with crime. Or all our entitlement spending that are drawing welfare seekers and driving our producers and job creators. The media is not interested in these facts. They are simply interested in pushing their narrative and destroying anyone who stands in their way. They sent a fake news journalist to find a way to distort the facts in order to make my campaign seem a certain way. What you are about to hear next is an absolutely disgusting account of how sick and twisted some in the liberal media are and how low they are willing to go to bring someone they disagree with down. The liberal mainstream media always claims to hold themselves to a high moral standard, especially when it comes to things such as calling out those who are pushing forth negative stereotypes about particular ethnic groups. Remember they are supposed to be the politically correct ones and we the conservatives are the backward, racist, xenophobic ones, right? I don't think so. What the CT Post and this rookie journalist did, in hopes to get her fifteen minutes of fame, was despicable. She wrote an article about myself, trying to characterize me as a crook. She also insinuated that I had ties to organized crime because of stereotypes that exist against people who work or live in this section of New York City where my business happens to be located and against those people who are born into particular ethnic groups that are common in this area. A clear act of liberal hypocrisy and shameful insinuation simply based off how I look and where my law practice is located. Imagine if a conservative publication had written a piece like this, insinuating something about someone of color simply because of where their business was located. They would suffer the most severe of consequences. They would be shunned from society as we know it. But because they were going after a white conservative, it is an acceptable thing. The young lady approached my campaign one day and had asked to do an interview, claiming that she was profiling all the major candidates in the race for governor. She asked me about everything from my campaign activities to my personal background to what I normally did for a living. After she had collected her information, she then took it upon herself to drive to my law offices in New York when I was not there and took photos of the outside of my office and the building that it was in, the surrounding offices, and the neighborhood. She then began to piece her propaganda together for the hit job she was about to unleash. A couple of weeks later, the piece came out. It was filled with all kinds of distortions and simply flat-out lies. She had used the imagery of the neighborhood where my office was located to paint a picture that I had a suspicious business, and that it had to be so, given the fact that it was in a particular kind of neighborhood where many Albanian and Italian Americans live. All this with no real facts concluding that I have anything to do with what she was insinuating. She claimed that my office was a front of some kind because there was no one there when she visited. She happened to visit my office on a day when I wasn't there because I was in court, but she didn't bother to say that. She just continued with her narrative. She called into question everything from the nature of my business dealings to my credentials as a lawyer, to the way I ran my campaign. Unfortunately her lies did have the effect of her intent, which was to have a negative impact on my campaign. Some of the delegates began to question me. It still amazes me how someone that you have known for multiple years would, all of a sudden, question your character simply because a fake news outlet published a fake news story. Which goes to show the power that the liberal media has in not just the state of Connecticut but all over the country. They hide behind the reputations that their publications once had, but far gone are the days when journalists were held accountable for their misdeeds in misreporting the facts and simply spreading false rumors and lies. And this journalist was able to get away with it unscathed. Not caring at all for the consequences of her lies and how it could have affected our campaign and my reputation as an individual. In fact she knew what she was doing either at her own device or under the device of her superiors at the CT Post as I said earlier. I reacted quickly though and gave a press conference a couple days after this article came out where I debunked every single one of her accusations with proof in hand for all her claims. The media was absolutely stunned when I chose to do this. They quickly ran out of questions, feeling the embarrassment they had drawn upon themselves by going on record and supporting the character of this fake news journalist who had done the hit piece on me. They very quickly realized that they had made a mistake by going after me because I would not relent in revealing their hypocrisy.

My opponents were joyed by news of this article making its rounds around the Republican political circles. And many, such as Tim Herbst's and Steve Obsitnik's campaign, were actively spreading the article among the delegates. Throughout the campaign, I probably received the most press coverage out of any candidate, but the amount of negative press coverage I received might have been double or triple what any other candidate received. Regardless, we carried on, and in the coming weeks, my fantastic team coordinated high-intensity ground operations. My field director Joe Hoxha worked relentlessly to identify and target delegates that had not committed, yet we would now spend every weekday and weekend, twelve hours or more a day on the road, having and attending meeting after meeting with delegations from all over the state. Brock Weber, my campaign manager, manned the office, coordinating phone banking operations in addition to doing his own private sit-downs with is leads. At this point, we were in full-on blitz mode. Although we had sustained some vicious attacks throughout the campaign thus far, most of our delegates that we had anticipated to retain were still with us. Now it was just a matter of building on that in order to secure the 15 percent at the convention in May that we needed in order to be on the primary ballot for August.

As the days dwindled down and months leading up to the convention had turned to weeks and weeks to days, candidates were making phone calls left and right, asking distinguished members of the party, elected officials, prominent names in the community, etc., for their endorsement. One of the most revered endorsement to get leading up to any kind of Republican contest is to have the endorsement of the leading Second Amendment organization in the state of Connecticut. This group is known as the Connecticut Citizens Defense League. It meant so much to me and my staff that I remember where I was and what I was doing the moment that I received that call from the president of the organization. We were coming back from an RTC meeting in the Northwest corner of the state, and I was receiving a call from Scott Wilson, the president of CCDL. Because there was limited cellular service in that area, I was not able to connect with him the first time. I remember feeling a little anxious and nervous knowing that this could be the moment that I know whether they have chosen me or someone else for the endorsement. The second time the phone rang, I was able to connect. Scott told me that he had good news and that I had won the executive boards' trust and that he was calling to congratulate me on receiving their endorsement for candidate for governor of Connecticut. I was thrilled. I knew that this was a huge plus leading up to the convention, and I truly was honored to have been given that endorsement. Receiving the CCDL endorsement did mean a lot to me because I truly felt that I was the best candidate when it came to the Second Amendment.

The time had finally come. It was the weekend of the convention. That morning we had one last RTC event before heading on out to the convention. The event was in Griswold, Connecticut. It was a small candidate forum, the last opportunity to change a few delegates minds. After having left the event with my field director, I get word from my campaign manager that Erin Stewart had decided she was going to drop out of the governor's race and run for lieutenant governor on the day of the convention. I must say she wasn't much of a political strategist because for the same reason, she wasn't going to get the nomination if she had stayed on to compete for governor. She wasn't going to get the party nomination for lieutenant governor either. The reason being is because she displayed no respect for the process either when she ran for governor or for lieutenant governor, for some reason, she was under the impression that she was going to be anointed lieutenant governor now that she wasn't going to compete for governor. Well, she was in for a rude awakening because the convention delegates did not appreciate her pure politically opportunistic tactic and thus did not reward her with the nomination that night. She did end up getting 15 percent to qualify for a primary but ended up losing badly in the primary.

When we arrived at the Foxwoods Casino, it felt almost like a calm before a storm. And that's exactly what it turned out to be. We spent that day up and down the convention floor, talking to delegates and doing counts all day. Today and tomorrow were the days where you had to work the hardest out of the whole campaign cycle. One unsquashed rumor that went unaddressed could ruin all the work that the campaign had put in throughout the year or, as in our case, years. We needed to stay on top of the delegates and make sure that we knew, to the highest possible degree of certainty, how many delegates we had and what percent that would equate to. At times we would go back up to our room in the hotel area and have a glass of wine and a cigar with some of the delegates, something that many of the delegates appreciated. That night we hosted a party at the room, where we had almost eighty people attend. It was probably the best moment of that convention for our campaign. Everyone was having a great time, and we felt confident that we had the votes that we needed heading into the next day. That night I don't know that anyone really got any sleep. After the party winded down, the prospects of what could happen later on that day became more and more looming. This was it. To me this was like the Super Bowl to a professional football player or like the coliseum to a gladiator in ancient Roman times. This was the moment that the campaign had been working toward all year. That morning we hosted a breakfast reception for all the delegates, and soon after the process of hounding, the delegates started again. The dress rehearsal was over, and now it was time to play for keeps. While the formalities of the convention were going on, my campaign and I were split a million different ways. At first you might have your sights set on a delegate that you don't quite have on board yet, and you are trying to talk them into voting for you if even just on a first ballot. Just when you got them to commit to you and you can add a plus 1 to your count, you would see one of your opponent's surrogates approaching one of your already identified delegates, and you would now need to go there and make sure your opponent did not sway them away from you. And don't forget that as soon as you left that person, you had to always keep one eye on him or her in case someone else tried to come along at some point. It was a constant game of cat and mouse, like a battle on the battlefield. At any moment, someone could come and blindside you. You trusted your core delegates but had to constantly verify, and in our case, we needed to add more. It was impossible to turn every stone. All the campaigns faced the same problem. It all just depended on how many delegates you knew you had and how much you needed if you didn't have enough. The biggest obstacle for us that night was a particular delegation that if we had on board, based off our projections, we would have had enough to reach the 15 percent threshold on a first ballot that we needed to qualify for the primary. Without them our chances would be a lot harder. At the last moment, the decision was given by those who decided where that delegation went, and the decision was that all this town's delegates would go to our campaign at least on a first ballot. Once we knew that, we could begin focusing on other delegations that needed to be addressed. The time had finally come, and the chairman was preparing to initiate the nomination process. My good friend and state representative Rob Sampson from Wolcott nominated me. I remember his nominating speech being very eloquent and powerful. The individual that seconded Rob's nomination was another state representative and friend of mine, Doug Dubitsky. His seconding speech was also very powerful. After everyone that was to be nominated was nominated, the process began and the delegations began to line up by congressional district starting with the second district and then by alphabetical order of your town. To my surprise, the betrayals occurred almost immediately. Delegates who had looked me in the eyes and promised they were going to vote for me on a first ballot did not do so, and we immediately began the ballot behind what we thought we would have. What that meant is that we were going to need to pick up delegates in areas where we were not expecting them. We did pick up such delegates, but after all the congressional districts went and after all the towns in those districts went, we were short by five or six votes to get the 15 percent we needed to automatically qualify for the primary. We did, however, make it to the second round or ballot, where this time we needed 15 percent, or we were out. Our campaign had projected that we weren't going to do as well in the second round as we would have in the first, meaning if we didn't get it in the first round, we weren't expecting to get in after the second. As the towns in their respective congressional districts started to line up again, we noticed very quickly that our momentum was even lower than the first ballot, as we expected. Toward the end, we reached about 145. More than twenty delegates short of the last round. However, there was one caveat. This time something known as switches were allowed. Meaning that after you had already cast your vote as a delegate, you had an opportunity to switch to a different candidate after everyone had already gone. During this time period, the room was completely chaotic. Deals were being struck, arguments being had, people moving to stretch, people moving to count votes, others to obstruct, candidates to beg. It was like a scene from the New York Stock Exchange on the day that the stock market crashed. I noticed that the delegation of the that town I was referring to earlier were huddled together looking like they were discussing something. They had promised only that they would vote for us on a first ballot, every single one of them, which they did. This time around, nothing was guaranteed, and this town's delegation had it written in their bylaws that they all would have to vote for the same candidate. But what they also said but did not promise was that if I could get within striking distance after the majority of switches were in, that they would switch their delegates back to us after having gone to our opponent Tim Herbst on the second ballot. Before the first congressional district switches were in, we had climbed back up to 161 delegate votes. Bristol switched two more to us, and if this last delegation whose identity I won't reveal had switched back to us, we would have qualified for the primary. However, a backroom deal was struck, and the delegates had already—under the direction of a very influential person from that town—ordered to hold firm in their support on this ballot for Tim Herbst. And just like that, the last of the few switches in the first congressional district were announced, and the ballot was declared closed, and once again, we had fallen less than a percentage point short of the threshold needed to qualify for the primary. The immediate aftermath was very anticlimactic. It was as if nothing had happened. A break was declared before the third ballot started, and there was nothing left to do anymore. We hadn't qualified for the primary. What had occurred didn't really hit me. Many people were surprised, thinking that I was one of the front-runners. I will have to admit, the feeling was very unpleasant. I truly felt betrayed, betrayed by those whom had given me their word, betrayed by some of those whom I had thought were my friends, and betrayed by the whole system that was working against me from day one—from the media and its distortions, to the dirty tactics employed by the other candidates. This was supposed to be a year where the Republican Party in Connecticut was going to come together for the sake of the future of the state. But it didn't seem that way. It seemed that almost every candidate that night, with the exception of Dave Walker, was willing to do anything and everything to win, selling out whatever they could sell out if it would give them even the slightest of advantages. I saw a lot more of this during the primary as I will discuss a little later on. As I was walking out with my campaign, David Stemerman, who was not nominated at this convention, approached me to talk about joining his campaign. He was going to run through the petition process. I agreed to speak with him at some point in the near future and left the convention hall as the third ballot was about to commence. In my room, I was accompanied by my close campaign staff. We went around the table and thanked each other for all the hard work that was put into the campaign. We had a terrific staff. We were very talented at what we did. We had a great relationship, and I was proud of my staff. We had been fighting a battle on multiple fronts for almost a year. No campaign given that kind of situation would have performed better than we did. We had experienced what it was like to be on the receiving end of the worst side of politics. The darkest side of politics. This wasn't going to be the year for us. The media loved it that I had lost. Reporters were paying more attention to me losing than Boughton winning. Everyone wanted a quote from me at that time. But just like in the victory four years ago when I was nominated for secretary of state by this party when I graciously accepted my nomination, I had to graciously accept my defeat and respect the will of the convention, even though it had been corrupted and compromised by backroom deals of quid pro quo and by my opponents who were spreading fake stories and lies about me. Many candidates' staff in addition to Stemerman approached me that night to ask for my endorsement, but I was not going to give it out that easily. Boughton ended up winning the convention and thus became the party-endorsed candidate. There had been much concern about Boughton's health leading up to the convention, with many speculating that the collapse he had at an event in Avon a few weeks prior could cost him the nomination at the convention. But apparently, the party establishment proved once again they weren't willing to try an outsider candidate and had chosen the establishment candidate, Mark Boughton.

In the weeks after the convention, I met with various candidates. Many sought my endorsement, including both Stemerman and Stefanowski, in addition to Tim Herbst and Mark Boughton. I couldn't support either of the convention candidates because of the dirty tricks they pulled at the convention. In addition, they were both way too liberal and way too wrong in how they thought Connecticut needed to be fixed. However, both Stemerman and Bob Stefanowski intrigued me. I sat down with both gentleman and decided that Stefanowski was a much-closer ideological fit for me than any other candidate left in the field. After about a couple of weeks or so, I had made it official. I had made a formal endorsement of Bob Stefanowski. I was the first major candidate to do so. I chose

Bob Stefanowski not only because we shared a lot of the same political thoughts on how to fix our state but because he came across as a genuine person who was serious about getting me involved in the primary and helping to bring the party together after the primary, should he be the winner. We were both optimistic about his chances in the primary. He was the most and truest conservative out of all the candidates remaining. And anyone who knows me well, knows that when I get behind someone to support them, I treat them as if it were myself. I fought hard for Bob. I pushed very hard to get him the CCDL endorsement that I had originally received before the convention myself. They ended up giving it to Tim Herbst, which was a disappointment for us considering that he had at one point received a D from the mother of all Second Amendment groups, the NRA. I believed that Bob should have received this endorsement, so a week or so before the primary, I did a robocall for him where I doubled down my support for him. This robocall was targeted to all the CCDL members in Connecticut and a lot of potential primary voters. In the robocall, I did say that I was the original endorsed candidate and as having had that endorsement, I wanted to double down on my endorsement of Bob Stefanowski for the primary and not Tim Herbst, who was now the endorsed candidate. I even called Tim a fake conservative, which to this day I still stand by those comments. Whether that had an effect or not, Bob performed really well in the debates and seemed like he was going to pull through as the winner of this primary.

When CCDL received word that I was not on board with their candidate, they moved to criticize me. The relationship became a little strained, but I told them that I could not support Tim and that I simply spoke what I truly believed to be the case about him, that he did not have a record to indicate that he was anywhere near what you would expect from someone who calls themselves a conservative. And I was not willing, not ever, to negotiate or comprise my principles, even if it meant not seeing eye to eye with CCDL, the organization that I still love and support to this day.

During this time, Mark Boughton and David Stemerman were hitting Bob hard, especially Stemerman. But Bob was not afraid to throw back and counterpunch, and he did just that. As primary day loomed, I remember thinking that the only thing that concerned me about the way that Bob Stefanowski was running his campaign was that he didn't have much of a field presence—no young kids knocking on doors and getting the vote out for him. This would not only be crucial for the primary, but it would be even more important for the general election if he were to win. I remember it being very important to my campaign in the general election campaign for secretary of state in 2014. It was one of the reasons why I was able to outperform Tom Foley, our candidate for governor back then in some towns and cities, because we had a strong and sustained field operation. By most indicators, including polling, Bob nonetheless seemed to be the front-runner. On primary day, I was invited to Bob's viewing party. I remember thinking that he was going to win. I had a good feeling about it, a strong feeling that tonight, we were going to be celebrating a win, and a win for a candidate who I thought was our best candidate and chance against Lamont and a third term of Dan Malloy.

That night when the numbers started coming in, Bob had pulled out in front from the beginning, and it remained that way for the rest of the night. When the final results came in, he had defeated Boughton at second place by eight points. Third place was Stemerman and fourth was Tim Herbst, trailing Stefanowski by thirteen points. That was truly a memorable night, and I am glad to have played a small role in Bob Stefanowski's primary win.

The general election was quite different, and this is where I am going to criticize Bob's campaign and the party as a whole.

In 2010, Tom Foley lost to Dan Malloy by around five thousand votes; in 2014, by nearly forty thousand votes; and in 2016, we gained enough state senate seats to have a tie in the Senate with the Democrats. Yet in 2018, we experienced dismal results. We lost by the same amount Foley lost in 2014 and slipped heavily into the minority in the state legislature, which was not a successful measure by any account. Although there was almost record-breaking turnout for both Republicans and Democrats, a strategy of just turning out Republicans won't work in a state like Connecticut where Democrats significantly outnumber Republicans. This year it had to be different. We needed to run a campaign that really spoke to the heart of what was ailing this state and how we could fix it. I believe that the message was right in terms of what we should have been telling people, but all the mechanisms were wrong. Connecticut is a very small but diverse state. Diverse in many ways. We have a lot of diversity of ideas, as well as all the different pockets of cultures and ethnic groups that are oftentimes overlooked in the political process by our party. Connecticut is also a geographically small state; a strong field program as is employed in many states around the country, some much bigger than Connecticut, would have been key to winning this general election. No such program was ever intended on being implemented in an effective way and in a timely manner. Lastly and arguably the most important thing was that the Republican Party and all its leaders never came together as one united force against the Democrats. Former candidates who had large constituencies did not do much to try and get the towns or cities they represented or currently represented to vote Republican this year. There were no rallies held by Mark Boughton or Mark Lauretti in Danbury and Shelton, respectively, two areas that could have certainly driven the vote out for Stefanowski. Danbury had gone Republican when Mark Boughton was on the ballot in 2010 for lieutenant governor. Turnout could have been higher in Trumbull and in Shelton. Glastonbury is always on the cusp of going Republican. Our elected officials from there could have swung that town because we do have Republican representation in Glastonbury. It wouldn't be out of the question. Instead, most of us were still bitter. No one besides a handful of party loyalists including myself really tried to do anything substantial for Bob Stefanowski in a general election. Mark Lauretti even tried to take the independent party line from Bob after the Republican primary. Only in Connecticut would politicians endorse someone and at the same time plot how to sabotage them. If Mark Lauretti had received the independent party line nomination, there would have been no way for Republicans to even have had a faint chance to win in November. The reason being is that most independents or unaffiliated lean Republican anyway, and our party's candidates' name on the independent line would have been key to a victory in the general election against Lamont, the democratic nominee. And it would have been that much more destructive to have the name of another Republican on the ballot that was not Bob Stefanowski. Mark should have really been ashamed of himself for attempting to do that. Being able to unify and really work hard for our candidate could have made all the difference we needed, bringing up turnout even higher in a few areas could have ate into the lead normally generated for the Democrats by the cities. Which brings me to my next point. During my campaign for governor, we stressed that we needed to do better in the cities, that it was not necessary to win the cities or even a plausible idea in today's political climate, but it was an area that we needed to work on. We needed to identify pockets in the cities where there are members of smaller ethnic groups—namely, Eastern Europeans such as in Hartford, New Britain, Waterbury, and Bridgeport. My campaign had identified these communities of having decent-sized populations of immigrants from former communist countries, mainly Eastern Europeans. This is an important fact because studies have shown time and time again that these groups, whether the Eastern Europeans in Connecticut or the Cuban Americans in South Florida, these people tend to be pretty conservative. The reason probably being that they would rather embrace a party that talks about freedom and limited government rather than one that wants to add more bureaucracy and government to their lives. Something that they are very weary and suspicious of, having left or in some cases escaped socialism or communism. These groups are always targeted by the Democrats, and when there is no one else competing for their attention and their votes, they naturally will go more toward the party that is paying more attention to them. You see, the Democrats are masters of not only coming together within their party after a primary, but they are masters at finding new voters to add to their coalitions. They are great coalition builders. A lot of that has to do with the fact that they are willing to say anything and everything just to get your vote. But bravo to them. They know how to win elections, at least here in Connecticut. None of this coalition building can be done, however, without a strong presence from the candidate himself in these communities. Walking the streets, knocking on doors with his or her staff, and appearing on local radio shows and local publications everywhere and anywhere. Unfortunately the core group Bob had were not willing to implement this strategy. It seemed to me that they were just there to collect a check and go back to their home states. His group didn't have the slightest clue about Connecticut politics, and that's because most of them weren't even from this state. They believed a cookie-cutter approach would work here, but unfortunately for the residents of this state, that approach didn't work. What we needed to win was the John Roland model from the last Republican that we had that could actually win the cities across multiple election cycles. He was very hardworking and a very relatable guy. But no one would have known that unless he did the hard work that he did, which was to go to the cities no matter how much his critics doubted him. We needed someone to tell the citizens why it is that Republican ideas and principles would benefit them. Unfortunately this old-school style of politics is not in favor anymore. Many great political victories have been attributed to a strong ground presence and strong field operations. Bill Clinton famously went to stores in the malls of New Hampshire greeting each person individually days before the New Hampshire primary. The retail style of politics was evidently missing from this campaign, and that, along with the fact that almost every other candidate failed to do anything substantial for Bob, is why we lost. Let's not forget about one more thing though—how Fairfield County really let Republicans down this time around. In 2014, we carried Greenwich by around a four-thousand-vote difference, and the same goes for a lot of the other Fairfield County towns. This time in some of those areas, we won by half that much or even in some cases lost straight out. And the state representatives and state senators in those areas also felt the dip in support. Many of whom lost their seats. It didn't come as a surprise to me at all that we performed that bad in Fairfield County. There was virtually no work done there by any campaign on our side. Assuming that because Republicans generally do well in that area, that they were going to do well in that area all the time. Forgetting that the dynamics of each election are different. It wasn't just the governor's campaign that didn't do much fieldwork down there, but all those legislators down there who lost failed to understand the importance of this election year. That with all the stuff going on in the media, we needed to get to the voters first and make sure that they remembered what were really the biggest issues in their lives and the mess that Connecticut was in and how we, as Republicans running for statewide offices and for seats in the legislature, were prepared to make things better for the people of Connecticut. We allowed the Democrats to beat us to the punch and let them make this campaign about national issues. In areas of the state like in Central and Eastern Connecticut where campaigns went out and knocked on doors early and made this election cycle about the local and state issues, they had a higher degree of success. It was easy to scapegoat Trump this election cycle, and it is easy to scapegoat our candidates as not having been good enough, but I think we as a party did not do good enough. We just didn't have the grassroots organization that has produced miracles for us all over the country at all levels—local, state and federal. We took certain things for granted and thus suffered the consequences All in all, this year was ours to lose, and we lost. I had been warning the candidates and party activists this time and time again, that given how unpopular the current governor was, we had a great opportunity to really make this a special election year and bring votes to the table from areas where we would not have thought possible four or eight years ago. We failed to do that, we failed to unite, and we failed to work hard, and that is why we lost. We have no one to blame but ourselves.

When Election Day finally came, everyone was excited. I honestly didn't know what to expect this time around. As I said before, I wasn't sure if we had done enough to win this. The initial returns that night came back strong for the Republicans, but I've been there and seen that before. Republicans always take the lead early on. Then when the cities come in, the lead begins to shrink. This time around, the Republicans were holding on until the late hours of the night, but again the cities had not come in. As local state rep and state senate races were being called, I could see that it wasn't looking promising. By midnight I had gotten word that not only did we not win the Senate, but we lost a few seats, thus sending us into the minority again. The same went for the House. What I did notice as some of the returns were coming in, certain communities were overperforming immensely for us. Cities and towns like Bristol and Plymouth and Naugatuck were all performing immensely for Bob and the Republicans. All these towns that I mentioned are blue-collar communities. Towns that also went for Trump two years ago. By the late morning the next day, Bob Stefanowski, seeing no more votes coming in from his areas, conceded the race to Ned Lamont. The results from the cities had finally come in, and just as an overnight nor'easter accumulates a foot and half of snow by the morning, so did Ned Lamont with a substantial forty-thousand-vote lead. We had gotten trounced yet again in the cities and in the wealthy suburbs. The only silver lining was that we had done better in the blue-collar manufacturing communities.

After nearly two years of hard-fought campaigning from everyone involved and a candidate who had bypassed the convention and beat the established candidates in the primary against all the odds, we the Republicans had managed to run out of steam just short of the end zone and failed once again. Ned Lamont, a wealthy businessman from Greenwich who has nothing in common with 99.99 percent of the voters, somehow convinced the Connecticut electorate that he knew what was best for them. That his continuation of Dan Malloy's policies were going to be what this state needed. Of course he never said it just like that, but that's exactly what he plans on doing, if not worse. He is already proposing tolls, new car taxes, and various consumption taxes on top of what we already have. Do these politicians really believe that that is the solution to the problems we face? Do they really believe that the reason that the nearly six hundred thousand people who have left Connecticut were all retirees that moved to Florida? Do they think this is just a joke? Or are they really that incompetent or worse, apathetic to the suffering of the people. Now I know Bob Stefanowski wasn't a perfect candidate. No one is. And I can assure you that I was far from perfect myself, but I believe that he really did want to make this state better and would have certainly made a better governor than Lamont. Any of our Republican candidates would make way better representatives and officials than anyone in today's Democratic Party, which seems to not have any regard for the workingman anymore. Their whole MO just seems to be tax and spend to make it seem like they're doing something, hoping that it will go on forever and that enough people will never notice the debt or the incrementally rising taxes. Republicans, for as mean as we can be to each other, we at least stand for something. We have a certain set of principles founded on logic and proven by history that when we are given a chance to govern in any capacity, most of us usually do a good job. The problem is, whether intentionally or not, whether out of bitterness and spite, or sometimes maybe even accidentally, we have a way of getting in each other's way when things don't go as planned for us on an individual level. That needs to stop. We need to stop the name-calling, the phony accusations, and the outright offensive and derogatory remarks toward each other. We need to learn how to unite. We almost didn't unite behind the president in 2016. It took a long time for some of us to realize that he was our nominee and that we needed to give him 110 percent, whether he was your first, second, or third choice. We all needed to do more for our ticket this election cycle. I helped out anyone and everyone on that ticket that I could. My friends and I did events for our terrific treasurer candidate Thad Gray. I campaigned and rallied for Bob Stefanowski. I donated to any and every Republican that I could. I never did anything to harm any Republican or the party. And as I said, for those of you out there who helped out any way that you could and didn't resort to dirty tactics to tear each other down, good for you. I know who those people are, and I am very grateful that I have had the chance to meet them and to get to know them, and keep setting a good example. For those out there who did not choose to unite, please let this be a lesson that in the future, we must help our fellow Republican, not tear them down because this time, it may be too late for our state.

Epilogue

Throughout previous empires, from antiquity to Victoria, the sustenance of imperial reign rested on perpetual war or expansion.

The American regime was always different.

The success of the Pax Romana under Augustus was nothing less than a counterinsurgency program devoted to exclusionary politics, an imperial act of delineating firm boundaries. The key to Roman order was to keep the empire within its bounds. For Augustus and his successors, the eight-hundred-year war of conquest was over. Augustus was sincere in his efforts to acknowledge that the pioneer work of continued advance against constantly opposing physical obstacles cannot go on forever. The task that Rome now had required a new framework. New ideas about the man and his place in the world was required if comity was to be found and order prevail. This mightier task was something Imperial Rome failed. Its agrarian ethics could not keep pace intellectually with the enormous advance embodied at the fringe of empire, a Judeo-Christian ethic that sundered the tribal night of archaism and obscurantism. What the Roman legions and its political class could not anticipate was the building of a new ethics, a new framework. A vision and an understanding not needed before is now imperative; the sources for Roman advance were now found on its deepest periphery.

The Roman oligarchy did not see that the old world had passed, and because no other men were capable of going forward to meet the march of events with new provisions, the imperium died, in a whimper.

The attributes of old were inadequate. The abilities of the pioneer and the conqueror, which had made empire, could not resolve the conditions brought forth from their achievements. To overcome nature or nations requires a distinct set of qualities, but the use of that victory as an enduring basis for a comity of order in human relations calls for different qualities. When nation-states must turn from extending the application of their efforts to the maintenance of wise use in self-negation, audacity and effort become useless. Effort based on the myopic vision of applied mass becomes a hindrance to progress. Arnold Toynbee's admonition was correct. The criteria for growth isn't expansion but self-determination. Roman ethics had no way to offer a resolution going forward. Rome's most enduring victories paled in comparison to the vision of man embodied in rival ethics on its periphery. The center simply couldn't hold.

We see identical problems in contemporary Western civilization, from pentagon acquisition reform to tax reform. Today's political order is based on confiscatory taxation. The entire social order is based on extraction of capital. It has reached its limit. There are rivalries ready to dismantle vestigial interests. This partially explains why politics has become so dreadful. Today's Democratic Party, and by consequence the GOP, has exhausted the citizenry. A look at our military leadership in Mesopotamia or our broken domestic entitlements reveal lost effigies to bygone eras. The resources advancing renewed civil society rest on the renewal of capital, human capital.

It is worth noting that the final reason for Rome's defeat was the failure of mind and spirit to rise to new opportunities, to master new challenges, and to be open to a new order of relations. For the ancients and previous imperial regimes, material progress was divorced from ethics; advancement simply outstripped human development.

Any look at our broken inner cities or exhausted individuals reveals a socialist dream of easily ameliorated dependent people. The atomization of human relations is a revolutionary goal. We now possess a broken, exhausted regime dependent on the extraction of capital for political cash transfers masquerading rent seeking.

Progressive ideology has reached its limit.

Let the counterrevolution begin.

About the Author

Peter Lumaj was born and raised in communist Albania. Peter graduated cum laude with a BA in political science from the City University of New York. He later attended Benjamin N. Cardozo School of Law. He is a small businessman, practicing attorney, and the owner of the Law Offices of Lumaj.

In 2014, Peter was selected the Republican nominee for Connecticut secretary of state where he is credited with running one of the closest races for statewide office in recent history in Connecticut. In 2018, he sought the nomination for governor in the state of Connecticut, where he fell short by three delegates.

He currently makes major media appearances as a Republican political strategist, including Fox News, FOX 61, i24NEWS, Sky News, etc.

Peter Lumaj resides in Fairfield, Connecticut. He is married to his wife, Mary, and they have three children: Frank, Amy, and Larisa.

CPSIA information can be obtained
at www.ICGtesting.com
Printed in the USA
LVHW021430260819
628944LV00006B/87/P